BURGERS

GOOD
HOUSEKEEPING

BURGERS

125 MOUTHWATERING RECIPES & TIPS

★ GOOD FOOD GUARANTEED ★

HEARST
books

HEARSTBOOKS

An Imprint of Sterling Publishing
1166 Avenue of the Americas
New York, NY 10036

ISBN 978-1-61837-201-7

GOOD HOUSEKEEPING
Jane Francisco
EDITOR IN CHIEF
Melissa Geurts
DESIGN DIRECTOR
Susan Westmoreland
FOOD DIRECTOR
Sharon Franke
FOOD APPLIANCES DIRECTOR

Cover Design: Scott Russo
Interior Design: Barbara Balch
Project Editor: Carol Prager

The Good Housekeeping Cookbook Seal guarantees that the recipes in this cookbook meet the strict standards
of the Good Housekeeping Research Institute. The Institute has been a source of reliable information and a
consumer advocate since 1900, and established its seal of approval in 1909. Every recipe has been triple-tested
for ease, reliability, and great taste.

www.goodhousekeeping.com

For information about custom editions, special sales, and premium and corporate purchases, please contact
Sterling Special Sales at 800-805-5489 or specialsales@sterlingpublishing.com.

Distributed in Canada by Sterling Publishing
c/o Canadian Manda Group, 664 Annette Street
Toronto, Ontario, Canada M6S 2C8
Distributed in Australia by Capricorn Link (Australia) Pty. Ltd.
P.O. Box 704, Windsor, NSW 2756, Australia

Manufactured in China

2 4 6 8 10 9 7 5 3 1

www.sterlingpublishing.com

CONTENTS

Smothered Swiss Turkey Burgers (page 88)

Foreword

If you were to create your perfect burger, what would it be? My go-to was classic California-style: Beef chuck, grilled medium-rare, with lettuce, tomato, and ketchup, no onion. That stack still makes me happy. But now that burgers have become a canvas for everything from Mexican to Vietnamese to pastrami spices, I find myself craving so many of the others in this book. Whether I'm topping a classic burger with caramelized onions and Gruyère for a rich riff on French Onion Soup, smearing chopped salmon burgers with a Cajun rémoulade, or mashing up beans with Mexican spices for a veggie burger, the possibilities are endless—and delicious. Along with over 80 recipes, you'll find tips on shaping, seasoning, cooking, safety, and more.

In the Good Housekeeping Test Kitchens, our team develops, triple-tests, and, yes, tastes every recipe that carries our name. For this book we tested to make sure these recipes work in any skillet or grill, with any brand of ingredients, no matter what. . . . So, get your heat on and start shaping those burgers!

SUSAN WESTMORELAND
Food Director, *Good Housekeeping*

Introduction

Whether "naked" (aka: unadorned) or piled high with "the works," nothing beats a hot, juicy burger. Succulence is a must for this citadel of American comfort food, whose cred is only worthy if it takes multiple napkins to polish one off. But let's be honest, there are many less-than-stellar burgers out there. Perhaps you've even been burned—literally—trying to make one. Here's the good news: this cookbook will not only show you how to make the best beef burger, but chicken, turkey, veggie, and everything in between.

What's the secret? It couldn't be simpler: the right fixings + proper technique = success. The first step is to "meat" your maker. Translation: the foundation of any hamburger is the meat. To get you started on the right track, follow our chart (see Ground Report, right) to pick the best meat for your burger. From there, we'll whip your patties into shape and offer sizzling cooking techniques that guarantee perfection. With must-have tips and recipes to flip for, we promise to make a burger meister out of you.

"MEAT" THE BUTCHER

Whatever burger you choose to make, we suggest using freshly ground meat if possible. Avoid packaged "hamburger," as it often contains ground scraps of questionable quality. Plus, once meat is compressed in a tray, it will never have the texture of a great burger. So if we're talking perfection, buy it freshly ground from a butcher you trust.

BURGERS SHAPE UP

The difference between a tough and tender burger isn't just the meat, but how you shape it into patties. Here's how:

1 Chill your hands under cold running water. Cold, wet hands help prevent the fat in the meat from melting, which can make burgers tough.

2 Handle the meat as little as possible. Working quickly, divide the meat into equal mounds and loosely shape into balls.

3 Gently flatten the balls into patties and smooth the edges all around. Don't overwork, squeeze, or compress the meat as you shape it or you'll end up with a dense burger.

4 Press into the centers of the patties with your thumbs to make deep indentations. Ground meat expands as it cooks, so these dents will prevent the burgers from puffing up during cooking. The result: a flat, beautifully shaped, cooked burger—perfect for piling on lots of toppings.

5 Stash the patties in the fridge until ready to cook (at least 30 minutes). Well-chilled patties will hold together better and cook more evenly.

BURGER LAB

A great burger also means a safe burger. Here are the ground rules you need to know:

- Keep ground meat refrigerated for up to 2 days in its supermarket wrap (or check the use-by date on the package). For longer storage, rewrap the meat in freezer wrap and freeze to use within 3 months.

- Don't allow raw patties or their juices to come in contact with other foods. If not cooking immediately, stack each patty with waxed paper or plastic wrap in between and place in an airtight container in the refrigerator. If transporting patties for a picnic, place the container in a cooler surrounded by ice packs.

- Use hot, soapy water to thoroughly wash any surfaces, hands, and utensils that come in contact with raw meat.

Ground Report

Our mandate for a great burger isn't complicated: for juiciness and best flavor, a little fat is your friend. We suggest relatively lean cuts of meat (80% to 90% lean) versus the very leanest, which contain almost no fat at all. The same rule applies when choosing ground chicken or turkey—go for both white and dark meat, not just breast. Let our chart be your guide to mouthwatering burgers.

MEAT	CUT	FLAVOR PROFILE	SAFE INTERNAL TEMPERATURE
Ground Beef	Chuck, 80%	Juicy, rich, bold, robust, hearty	160°F (medium doneness)
Ground Lamb	Shoulder	Unique, full-flavored, firm texture, aromatic	160°F (medium doneness)
Ground Pork	Butt	Delicate, mild, good alternative to beef and poultry	160°F (medium doneness)
Ground Chicken	Thigh and Breast, 85% to 90% lean	Lean, light texture, tender, subtle flavor, excellent choice for add-ins and toppings	165°F (well-done)
Ground Turkey	Thigh and Breast, 85% to 90% lean	Moist, delicate flavor, denser texture than chicken	165°F (well-done)

- Cook all burgers thoroughly. Beef, pork, and lamb burgers don't have to be well-done to be safe—just not rare. However, chicken and turkey burgers need to be thoroughly cooked. Cooking times for burgers will vary, depending on the thickness of the patties and the type of heat used.
- Always test burgers for doneness. Insert an instant-read thermometer horizontally into the center of each burger to get a reading in seconds (see Ground Report, page 9, for safe internal temperatures).

GRILL SMARTS

There's little argument that a grilled burger with a perfectly charred crust and juicy interior is marked for greatness. Follow these steps for superbly cooked burgers every time. (Same rules apply for a grill pan; see A Pan and a Grill Plan, opposite.)

1 Get the grill rack good and hot before putting on the burgers. That way, they won't stick. Note: When grilling very lean ground meat, poultry, or fish, it's a good idea to spray both

sides of the patties with a nonstick cooking spray or lightly brush them with vegetable oil before cooking.

2 Season burgers with salt at the last minute, as salt draws out moisture from ground meat immediately upon contact. Not a good thing for a juicy burger.

3 Never flatten or score burgers with a spatula while cooking or you'll lose precious juices.

4 Turn burgers only once; any more often and you'll run the risk of tearing the surface before it has the chance to turn into a tasty crust.

5 Give cooked burgers a rest before serving. A few minutes will allow the juices to redistribute throughout the burger. If you cut into a burger right away, the juices will run out onto the plate—instead of inside your mouth.

A PAN AND A GRILL PLAN

Serious burger lovers, consider this: when you add a grill pan to your cooking arsenal, a mouthwatering, chargrilled burger transforms from a seasonal outdoor treat to a stovetop year-round indulgence. A grill pan is essentially a skillet with ridges on the bottom. Grill pans come in a wide range of sizes, including griddle-style pans without sides. They're built for cooking over two stovetop burners at once, and are very useful when you're cooking food for more than two people. You also have your choice of materials, from the classic cast-iron and enamelled cast-iron to stainless steel and hard-anodized aluminum. One thing to consider when purchasing a grill pan is whether you want a stay-cool handle. If you opt for one without that feature, please remember that the handle will get just as hot as the rest of the pan,

so don't absentmindedly grab it—you'll end up with a nasty burn.

Skip grill pans with a nonstick coating; these should not be preheated empty, and if they are heated over more than medium heat, the coating can begin to degrade, releasing harmful chemicals. Our pick for burgers? A preseasoned cast-iron grill pan. All that's required for cleaning is a rinse in hot water—no detergent, as that can remove the seasoning. Immediately dry your pan, then rub it with a light coating of vegetable oil (just enough to restore the sheen without being sticky).

BEST BUNS

Now that we've covered burgers, let's not forget the buns. There's a lot to be said about soft buns (versus artisanal rolls, which can break up your burger). Spend the extra coin and choose good quality buns, those with enough texture not to disintegrate under a juicy burger. Sesame, whole wheat, whole-grain, and potato buns are all good supermarket options. Or splurge with buttery brioche hamburger buns. Finally, take a few moments to lightly toast the buns on the grill or under the broiler. It really amps up the flavor—another essential part of a mind-blowing burger.

Our Best Burger
(page 14)

1 | Build a Burger

When it comes to making a fabulous burger, we're purists: start with the best meat, use the right heat, add salt and pepper, then serve on a toasted bun, and you're good to go. We keep it simple with two master recipes: Our Best Burger (page 14) and its trendy sidekick—the slider.

With burger toppings, a cook has the chance to let loose. So when it's time to build an even more fabulous burger, take our ultimate beef burger and transform it into something deliciously exotic, like Vietnamese Bánh Mì Burgers (page 18) or Chips 'n' Guac Burgers (page 18). For gourmet burgers in mere minutes, grab a jar of mayo and whip up a trio of creamy spreads (page 29). And if you're thinking party food, our Classic Sliders (page 25) can be made with ground beef, pork, chicken, or turkey, and we even offer five amazing spin-off recipes to choose from.

Our Best BURGER

Hankering for the ultimate burger recipe?
Your search is officially over! Choose from our collection of
Fresh Fixings to slather on top (right) or enjoy six fabulous
spin-off recipes (pages 18–20). For photo, see page 12.

ACTIVE TIME: 10 MINUTES   **TOTAL TIME:** 18 MINUTES
MAKES: 4 BURGERS

1¼ **pounds ground beef chuck**

¾ **teaspoon salt**

½ **teaspoon coarsely ground black pepper**

4 **hamburger buns, split**

lettuce leaves, for topping

sliced tomato, for topping

South of the Border topping (page 15), optional

1 Divide ground beef into 4 mounds (about
5 ounces each), and loosely shape into balls.

2 Using your hands, gently flatten balls into
¾-inch-thick patties, handling meat as little as
possible. Smooth patty edges with your fingers.

3 Place patties on a flat surface. Using your
thumbs, press into the centers of patties to make
deep indentations. Refrigerate until ready to grill.

4 Prepare outdoor grill for direct grilling over
medium-high heat, or heat ridged grill pan over
medium-high heat until very hot. Sprinkle salt
and pepper on both sides of patties.

5 Place patties on hot grill rack. Cook 8 to 12
minutes for medium, or until desired doneness
is reached, turning over once. About 1 minute
before burgers are done, add buns, cut sides
down, to grill rack. Grill just until toasted.

6 Serve burgers on buns with lettuce, tomato,
and South of the Border topping, if using.

EACH SERVING (WITHOUT TOPPINGS): ABOUT 378
CALORIES, 29G PROTEIN, 21G CARBOHYDRATE,
19G TOTAL FAT (7G SATURATED), 1G FIBER, 85MG
CHOLESTEROL, 718MG SODIUM.

TIP

Use a long-handled spatula with a heatproof
handle to easily flip the patties on the grill.

Fresh Fixings

Give Our Best Burger (opposite) megawatt taste
with these almost-instant toppers. All recipes serve 4.

GINGERY MAYO

Stir together **½ cup mayonnaise, 2 table-spoons Sriracha, 2 teaspoons soy sauce,** and **1 teaspoon grated, peeled fresh ginger** until blended. Makes about ⅓ cup.

EACH SERVING: ABOUT 587 CALORIES, 29G PROTEIN, 23G CARBOHYDRATE, 41G TOTAL FAT (10G SATURATED), 1G FIBER, 95MG CHOLESTEROL, 1,195MG SODIUM.

REUBEN

Stir together **⅓ cup mayonnaise; ¼ cup sauerkraut,** chopped; **2 tablespoons relish; 1 tablespoon ketchup; 1 tablespoon spicy brown mustard;** and **¼ teaspoon garlic powder.** Serve on burgers with **4 slices (1 ounce each) melted Swiss cheese.** Makes ¾ cup.

EACH SERVING: ABOUT 637 CALORIES, 37G PROTEIN, 27G CARBOHYDRATE, 41G TOTAL FAT (14G SATURATED), 1G FIBER, 117MG CHOLESTEROL, 1,053MG SODIUM.

MANGO TANGO

Combine **2 ripe mangoes,** peeled and finely chopped; **¼ cup fresh cilantro leaves,** chopped; **1 small shallot,** finely chopped; **2 tablespoons orange juice;** and **¼ teaspoon salt** until blended. Makes 2⅓ cups.

EACH SERVING: ABOUT 485 CALORIES, 31G PROTEIN, 48G CARBOHYDRATE, 19G TOTAL FAT (7G SATURATED), 4G FIBER, 85MG CHOLESTEROL, 794MG SODIUM.

SOUTH OF THE BORDER

Divide **1 ripe, lightly mashed avocado, ¼ cup crumbled Cotija or feta cheese,** and **16 slices pickled jalapeño** among 4 cooked burgers. Makes 1½ cups.

EACH SERVING: ABOUT 487 CALORIES, 32G PROTEIN, 26G CARBOHYDRATE, 28G TOTAL FAT (9G SATURATED), 5G FIBER, 92MG CHOLESTEROL, 874MG SODIUM.

Coal Country

Have a charcoal grill? Use our thumb sheet
and you'll make sizzling good burgers every time.

LIGHT THE BARBIE

While gas and electric grills are easy to light, starting a charcoal fire requires a little more finesse. Here are the basics:

1 Leave yourself time after starting the fire. The coals need to develop a light layer of ash before you start cooking. Allow for 20 minutes to be on the safe side.

2 Start with enough briquettes. You don't want to run out of heat before your burgers are done. Estimate the right amount of briquettes by spreading an even layer over the bottom of the firebox.

3 Before lighting, stack the coals into a pyramid. This will allow air to circulate so the coals will quickly ignite.

FIRE STARTERS

To get the charcoal fire going for your burgers, you have options:

- **Chimney starter:** This is an open-ended metal cylinder with a handle. Stuff crumpled newspaper in the bottom, fill the top portion with briquettes, and then light the paper through an opening in the bottom. The briquettes will burn to ash-covered readiness.

- **Electric starter:** Place this loop-shaped, handled heating element in a bed of briquettes, plug it in, and the briquettes will ignite.

- **Liquid fire starter:** Saturate briquettes with the liquid, and then wait for a minute before lighting. By the time the coals are ready for proper cooking, the fluid will have burned off and will not affect the flavor of the food. Never add liquid starter to a fire that's already burning or to hot coals; a spark could ignite the whole can.

- **Solid fire starter:** Place these waxy-looking cubes in the firebox, pile briquettes on top, and light. They're safer to handle than liquid starter.

- **Self-starting briquettes:** These are impregnated with starter fluid. A match will ignite them immediately. Don't add them to a fire that's already lit.

HOW HOT IS THE FIRE?

You'll know the coals are ready when they are about 80 percent ashy gray (at night, you'll see them glow red). To test the level of heat, hold your palm above the coals at cooking height (about 6 inches). If you can keep your palm over the fire for just 2 to 3 seconds, the fire is hot; 4 to 5 seconds, the fire is medium; 5 to 6 seconds, the fire is low.

TIP

Tapping the coals will remove their ash cover and make the fire hotter. Pushing the coals together intensifies the heat; spreading them apart decreases it. Opening the vents on a covered grill increases the temperature, and partially closing them lowers the heat.

Extra-Extra BURGERS!

Start with Our Best Burger recipe (page 14),
and then choose from these lip-smacking spin-offs.

Chips 'n' Guac
BURGERS

Prepare Our Best Burgers. Serve burgers as in
step 6, but omit lettuce, tomato, and optional
topping. Top burgers evenly with **¼ cup
guacamole**, **¼ cup sliced pickled jalapeños**,
and **14 tortilla chips**.

....

EACH SERVING: ABOUT 435 CALORIES, 30G PROTEIN,
27G CARBOHYDRATE, 22G TOTAL FAT (7G SATURATED),
3G FIBER, 85MG CHOLESTEROL, 871MG SODIUM.

Vietnamese Bàhn Mì
BURGERS

In medium bowl, mix **1 medium Kirby
cucumber**, sliced; **¼ cup shredded carrots**;
2½ tablespoons seasoned rice vinegar;
2 tablespoons fresh mint leaves, chopped; and
¼ teaspoon salt; cover and refrigerate 1 hour.
Prepare Our Best Burgers. Serve burgers as in
step 6, but omit lettuce, tomato, and optional
topping. Top burgers evenly with cucumber
mixture.

....

EACH SERVING: ABOUT 399 CALORIES, 29G PROTEIN,
26G CARBOHYDRATE, 19G TOTAL FAT (7G SATURATED),
1G FIBER, 85MG CHOLESTEROL, 1,132MG SODIUM.

Island
BURGERS

Prepare Our Best Burgers. Serve burgers as in step 6, but omit lettuce, tomato, and optional topping. Top burgers evenly with **½ cup shredded pepper Jack cheese**; **1 green onion**, thinly sliced; and **4 fresh pineapple rings**.

....

EACH SERVING: ABOUT 463 CALORIES, 32G PROTEIN, 29G CARBOHYDRATE, 23G TOTAL FAT (9G SATURATED), 2G FIBER, 100MG CHOLESTEROL, 806MG SODIUM.

Spicy Elvis
BURGERS

Prepare Our Best Burgers. Serve burgers as in step 6, but omit lettuce, tomato, and optional topping. Divide **¾ cup crunchy peanut butter** and **½ cup hot pepper jelly** among burgers. Top burgers evenly with **8 slices cooked bacon** (2 slices per burger).

....

EACH SERVING: ABOUT 817 CALORIES, 46G PROTEIN, 50G CARBOHYDRATE, 49G TOTAL FAT (13G SATURATED), 5G FIBER, 102MG CHOLESTEROL, 1,236MG SODIUM.

Extra-Extra BURGERS!

Crunchy Onion
BURGERS

Prepare Our Best Burgers. Serve burgers as in
step 6, but omit lettuce, tomato, and optional
topping. Top burgers evenly with **¼ cup onion
dip** and **1 cup canned fried onions** (we love
French's®).

....

EACH SERVING: ABOUT 495 CALORIES, 31G PROTEIN,
28G CARBOHYDRATE, 28G TOTAL FAT (10G SATURATED),
1G FIBER, 85MG CHOLESTEROL, 912MG SODIUM.

Sriracha-Mayo
BURGERS

Prepare Our Best Burgers. Serve burgers as in
step 6, but omit lettuce, tomato, and optional
topping. Mix together **1 cup mayonnaise; ½ cup
sour cream; 4 grilled green onions**, chopped;
**1½ tablespoons Sriracha; 1 teaspoon honey;
1 teaspoon lemon juice; ⅛ teaspoon salt;** and
⅛ teaspoon pepper. Divide among burgers.

....

EACH SERVING: ABOUT 840 CALORIES, 30G PROTEIN,
26G CARBOHYDRATE, 68G TOTAL FAT (16G SATURATED),
1G FIBER, 117MG CHOLESTEROL, 1,277MG SODIUM.

Smoky Barbecue
BURGERS

A double dose of barbecue sauce—in the patties
and slathered on top—is the secret to these extra-juicy burgers.

ACTIVE TIME: 15 MINUTES   TOTAL TIME: 23 MINUTES

MAKES: 4 BURGERS

1¼ pounds ground beef chuck

½ cup barbecue sauce

2 green onions, chopped

1 tablespoon chopped jalapeño chile

½ teaspoon salt

4 hamburger buns, split and toasted

1 Prepare outdoor grill for direct grilling over medium heat.

2 In medium bowl, combine ground beef, ¼ cup barbecue sauce, green onions, jalapeño, and salt until blended, but do not overmix.

3 Shape meat mixture into 4 equal patties, each about ¾-inch thick, handling meat as little as possible.

4 Place patties on hot grill rack; cook 4 minutes. Turn burgers over and brush with remaining ¼ cup barbecue sauce; cook 4 to 6 minutes longer for medium, or until desired doneness is reached. Serve burgers on buns.

....

EACH SERVING: ABOUT 438 CALORIES, 29G PROTEIN, 36G CARBOHYDRATE, 19G TOTAL FAT (7G SATURATED), 1G FIBER, 85MG CHOLESTEROL, 923MG SODIUM.

TIP

For an even bigger blast of flavor, use hickory or honey barbecue sauce.

Just Pickled

Love pickles with your burger?
Our DIY recipe and pretty-in-pink onions
take only minutes to prep.

QUICK PICKLES

In freezer-weight resealable plastic bag, combine **¾ cup distilled white vinegar**, **¼ cup water**, **4 teaspoons sugar**, **½ teaspoon salt**, **¼ cup chopped fresh dill**, and **½ teaspoon whole black peppercorns**. Add **2 pounds Kirby (pickling) cucumbers**, quartered lengthwise. Seal bag and refrigerate at least overnight, or up to 1 week. Makes about 40 pickles.

....

EACH PICKLE: ABOUT 4 CALORIES, 0G PROTEIN, 1G CARBOHYDRATE, 0G TOTAL FAT, 0G FIBER, 0MG CHOLESTEROL, 9MG SODIUM.

SWEET & TANGY ONIONS

Peel **6 medium red onions** (about 1½ pounds); cut each into 6 wedges, leaving a little of the root end to help hold shape during cooking. In large skillet, heat onions, **½ cup water**, **½ cup sugar**, and **1 teaspoon salt** to boiling over high heat. Reduce heat to low; cover and simmer 3 to 5 minutes or until onions are tender-crisp. Transfer onion mixture to medium bowl; cover and refrigerate until chilled for best flavor. Makes about 4 cups.

....

EACH ½-CUP SERVING: ABOUT 80 CALORIES, 1G PROTEIN, 21G CARBOHYDRATE, 0G TOTAL FAT, 3G FIBER, 0MG CHOLESTEROL, 270MG SODIUM.

Classic SLIDERS

What could be better than a big, ultra-juicy
GH Best Burger? Several equally fabulous tiny burgers
made with beef, pork, chicken, or turkey—
plus delicious variations (pages 26-27).

ACTIVE TIME: 10 MINUTES   TOTAL TIME: 15 MINUTES
MAKES: 12 SLIDERS

1¼ pounds ground beef chuck, pork, lamb,
    chicken, or turkey

¾   teaspoon salt

½   teaspoon ground black pepper

12 slider mini buns, split and toasted

plum tomato slices, small lettuce leaves, dill
    pickle slices, and/or onion slices (optional)

1 Prepare outdoor grill for direct grilling over
medium heat.

2 Shape ground beef into 12 equal patties, each
½-inch thick, handling meat as little as possible.
Sprinkle salt and pepper on both sides of patties.

3 Place patties on hot grill rack; cook 5 to 6
minutes for medium, or until desired doneness is
reached, turning over once.

4 Serve burgers on buns with tomato, lettuce,
pickles, and onion, if using.

EACH SLIDER: ABOUT 145 CALORIES, 10G PROTEIN, 9G
CARBOHYDRATE, 8G TOTAL FAT (3G SATURATED), 1G
FIBER, 32MG CHOLESTEROL, 240MG SODIUM.

TIP

If preparing these sliders with ground
chicken or turkey, make sure to spray both
sides of the patties with nonstick cooking
spray and increase the cooking time to 6 to
7 minutes.

Super SLIDERS!

It's so easy! Take our Classic Sliders recipe (page 25),
and then select from five sensational variations.

Ranch
SLIDERS

Prepare Classic Sliders with ground chicken or
turkey, but in step 2, before shaping patties,
mix **1 medium carrot**, shredded (about ½ cup);
1 green onion, chopped; and **¼ cup ranch salad
dressing** with ground meat until blended, but
do not overmix. Sprinkle patties with pepper but
not salt. Serve burgers as in step 4, but spoon
additional ranch dressing over burgers, if desired.

....

EACH SLIDER: ABOUT 140 CALORIES, 10G PROTEIN, 10G
CARBOHYDRATE, 8G TOTAL FAT (0G SATURATED), 1G
FIBER, 0MG CHOLESTEROL, 150MG SODIUM.

Corn & Salsa
SLIDERS

Prepare Classic Sliders with ground chicken
or turkey, but in step 2, before shaping patties,
mix **½ cup fresh or frozen (thawed) corn
kernels** and **¼ cup medium salsa** with meat
mixture until blended, but do not overmix. Do
not sprinkle patties with salt and pepper. At the
end of step 3, place slices of **pepper Jack cheese**
(about 4 ounces total) on top of burgers; cover
grill and cook until cheese melts, about 1 minute.
Serve burgers as in step 4, but spoon additional
medium salsa over burgers, if desired.

....

EACH SLIDER: ABOUT 160 CALORIES, 12G PROTEIN, 11G
CARBOHYDRATE, 8G TOTAL FAT (3G SATURATED), 1G
FIBER, 10MG CHOLESTEROL, 170MG SODIUM.

Teriyaki
SLIDERS

Prepare Classic Sliders with ground beef, pork, chicken, or turkey, but in step 2, before shaping patties, mix **½ cup diced water chestnuts, ¼ cup teriyaki sauce**, and **¼ teaspoon crushed red pepper** with meat until blended, but do not overmix. Do not sprinkle patties with salt and pepper. Serve burgers as in step 4, but spoon **¼ cup hoisin sauce** evenly over burgers.

....

EACH SLIDER: ABOUT 165 CALORIES, 11G PROTEIN, 13G CARBOHYDRATE, 8G TOTAL FAT (3G SATURATED), 1G FIBER, 32MG CHOLESTEROL, 410MG SODIUM.

Pesto
SLIDERS

Prepare Classic Sliders with ground chicken, turkey, pork, or beef, but in step 2, before shaping patties, mix **¼ cup refrigerated or jarred pesto** with meat until blended, but do not overmix. Sprinkle patties with salt and pepper. Serve burgers as in step 4, but spoon additional pesto over burgers, if desired.

....

EACH SLIDER: ABOUT 140 CALORIES, 10G PROTEIN, 9G CARBOHYDRATE, 8G TOTAL FAT (3G SATURATED), 1G FIBER, 10MG CHOLESTEROL, 270MG SODIUM.

Rosemary-Cabernet
SLIDERS

Prepare Classic Sliders with ground beef or lamb, but in step 2, before shaping patties, mix **⅓ cup Cabernet Sauvignon** or other dry red wine and **2 teaspoons finely chopped fresh rosemary** with meat until blended, but do not overmix. Sprinkle patties with salt and pepper. Serve burgers as in step 4.

....

EACH SLIDER: ABO CALORIES, 11G PROTEIN, 9G CARBOHYDRATE, 8G TOTAL FAT (3G SATURATED), 1G FIBER, 32MG CHOLESTEROL, 240MG SODIUM.

Day-O Mayo!

Hold the ketchup! Grab a jar of mayo and slather
your next burger or slider with one of these creamy toppers instead.
All recipes serve 4 (or make enough for 12 sliders).

ONION-THYME MAYO

Prepare outdoor grill for direct grilling
over medium heat. Cut **1 medium onion**
crosswise into ½-inch-thick rounds. Place
onion slices on hot grill rack and cook
until tender and browned on both sides,
8 to 10 minutes, turning over once.
Transfer onion to cutting board; coarsely
chop. Place onion in small serving bowl;
stir in **¼ cup light mayonnaise** and
1 teaspoon chopped fresh thyme leaves
until blended. Makes about ½ cup.

. . . .

EACH TABLESPOON: ABOUT 30 CALORIES,
0G PROTEIN, 2G CARBOHYDRATE, 3G TOTAL FAT
(1G SATURATED), 0G FIBER, 3MG CHOLESTEROL,
60MG SODIUM.

HORSERADISH-MUSTARD MAYO

In small serving bowl, stir together
**¼ cup light mayonnaise, 1 tablespoon
undrained, prepared white horseradish**,
and **2 teaspoons Dijon mustard with
seeds** until blended. Makes about ⅓ cup.

. . . .

EACH TABLESPOON: ABOUT 45 CALORIES,
0G PROTEIN, 1G CARBOHYDRATE, 4G TOTAL FAT
(1G SATURATED), 0G FIBER, 4MG CHOLESTEROL,
105MG SODIUM.

. . . .

BACON-CHIPOTLE MAYO

Place **2 slices bacon** on paper towel–
lined, microwave-safe plate. Cover with
paper towel. Cook bacon in microwave on
high until well browned, 1½ to 2 minutes.
Cool bacon until crisp. Crumble bacon;
place in small serving bowl. Stir in **¼ cup
light mayonnaise** and **1 teaspoon canned
chipotle chile puree** (adobo). Puree until
blended. Makes about ⅓ cup.

. . . .

EACH TABLESPOON: ABOUT 55 CALORIES, 1G
PROTEIN, 1G CARBOHYDRATE, 5G TOTAL FAT
(1G SATURATED), 0G FIBER, 6MG CHOLESTEROL,
135MG SODIUM.

Mediterranean Spiced
Burgers (page 34)

2 | Over-the-Top Burgers

It's time to leave your daddy's ho-hum patties in the dust and say hello to our collection of over-the-top burgers. Prime picks for beef include heavenly Pastrami Burgers (page 33), Steakhouse Burgers with Horseradish Sour Cream (page 35), or—in our humble opinion—the best BLT Burgers you'll ever sink your teeth into (page 38). Or, if you haven't tried a lamb burger before, our Mediterranean Spiced Burgers (page 34) and Greek Lamb Burgers (page 47) will introduce you to a whole new level of succulence.

Seasonings like onions, ketchup, and Worcestershire sauce not only make our Meatloaf Burgers with Sautéed Carrots (page 42) tastier, they also add juiciness. Before shaping the patties, mix in seasonings as gently as possible with your fingertips so you don't compress the texture. If time allows, chill the meat mixture again before shaping to allow the flavors to meld.

Pastrami
BURGERS

A deli classic gets a serious upgrade
with these ultra-juicy spiced burgers
slathered with mustard and served on rye.

ACTIVE TIME: 10 MINUTES   **TOTAL TIME:** 18 MINUTES
MAKES: 4 BURGERS

2   teaspoons ground coriander

2   teaspoons paprika

1½ teaspoons ground ginger

½   teaspoon sugar

¼   teaspoon cayenne (ground red) pepper

1   teaspoon salt

2   teaspoons coarsely ground black pepper

1¼ pounds ground beef chuck

8   oval slices rye bread with caraway seeds

deli mustard, for topping

1   Prepare outdoor grill for direct grilling over medium heat.

2   In cup, combine coriander, paprika, ginger, sugar, cayenne pepper, salt, and black pepper.

3   Shape ground beef into 4 oval patties, each about ½-inch thick, handling meat as little as possible. On waxed paper, pat spice mixture onto both sides of patties.

4   Place patties on hot grill rack; cook 8 to 9 minutes for medium, or until desired doneness is reached, turning over once.

5   Serve burgers on rye bread with mustard.

....

EACH SERVING: ABOUT 485 CALORIES, 31G PROTEIN, 33G CARBOHYDRATE, 24G TOTAL FAT (9G SATURATED), 4G FIBER, 96MG CHOLESTEROL, 1,095MG SODIUM.

TIP

Don't be shy when seasoning your burgers with coarsely ground black pepper. Not only does it give burgers a robust taste, its coarse texture makes for a fabulous grilled crust.

Mediterranean
SPICED BURGERS

Talk about taste—these sophisticated burgers with cilantro, coriander, and garlic are topped with grilled onion, feta cheese, and curry-spiked ketchup. For photo, see page 30.

ACTIVE TIME: 15 MINUTES   **TOTAL TIME:** 23 MINUTES
MAKES: 4 BURGERS

1   pound ground meat (lamb, beef, or turkey)

½   cup packed fresh cilantro leaves, finely chopped

2   cloves garlic, crushed with garlic press

1   teaspoon ground coriander

¼   teaspoon salt

1   medium red onion, cut into ½-inch rounds

4   hamburger buns, split

⅓   cup ketchup

1   teaspoon curry powder

2   tablespoons crumbled feta cheese

fresh cilantro sprigs, for topping

1   Prepare outdoor grill for direct grilling over medium-high heat.

2   In medium bowl, combine ground meat, cilantro, garlic, and coriander until blended, but do not overmix. Shape meat mixture into 4 equal patties, each about ¼-inch thick, handling meat as little as possible. Sprinkle salt on both sides of patties. (For ground turkey, spray both sides of patties with nonstick cooking spray.)

3   Place patties and onion slices on hot grill rack; cook 8 to 10 minutes for medium, or until desired doneness is reached, turning over once (onions should be browned and tender). About 1 minute before burgers are done, add buns, cut sides down, to grill. Grill just until toasted.

4   Meanwhile, in small bowl, stir together ketchup and curry powder until blended.

5   Serve burgers on buns with curry ketchup, feta, onion, and cilantro sprigs.

EACH SERVING: ABOUT 387 CALORIES, 25G PROTEIN, 31G CARBOHYDRATE, 18G TOTAL FAT (7G SATURATED), 2G FIBER, 79MG CHOLESTEROL, 667MG SODIUM.

TIP

Shape the patties up to 3 hours before grilling, but hold the salt until the last second.

Steakhouse Burgers
WITH HORSERADISH SOUR CREAM

Top these juicy burgers with our creamy
homemade horseradish sauce for a
powerful punch of flavor.

ACTIVE TIME: 15 MINUTES   TOTAL TIME: 21 MINUTES
MAKES: 4 BURGERS

1¼ pounds ground beef chuck

salt

coarsely ground black pepper

⅓ cup sour cream

2½ teaspoons prepared white horseradish

4   English muffins, split and lightly toasted

4   Boston lettuce leaves

1 Lightly spray ridged grill pan or skillet with
nonstick cooking spray, and heat over medium-
high heat until hot.

2 Shape ground beef into 4 equal patties, each
about ½-inch thick, handling meat as little as
possible. Sprinkle ½ teaspoon salt and 1 teaspoon
pepper on both sides of patties, pressing pepper
lightly into patties.

3 Place patties in hot grill pan; cook about
6 minutes for medium, or until desired doneness
is reached, turning over once.

4 Meanwhile, in small bowl, stir together
sour cream, horseradish, ⅛ teaspoon salt, and
⅛ teaspoon pepper until blended.

5 Serve patties on English muffins with lettuce
leaves and horseradish sauce.

....

EACH SERVING: ABOUT 505 CALORIES, 32G PROTEIN,
31G CARBOHYDRATE, 27G TOTAL FAT (11G SATURATED),
0G FIBER, 104MG CHOLESTEROL, 880MG SODIUM.

Classic
OVEN FRIES

It wouldn't be the ultimate burger without a side of crispy fries. Our fabulous recipe has 2 tasty spin-offs for continued combos.

ACTIVE TIME: 15 MINUTES   TOTAL TIME: 40 MINUTES
MAKES: 4 SERVINGS

- 2 tablespoons olive oil
- 3 medium baking potatoes (about 8 ounces each)
- 3/4 teaspoon salt
- 1/4 teaspoon coarsely ground black pepper

1 Place 2 oven racks in upper and lower thirds of oven. Preheat oven to 425°F. Brush 2 large cookie sheets with 1 tablespoon oil.

2 Cut each unpeeled potato lengthwise into quarters, then cut each quarter lengthwise into 2 wedges (or, cut potatoes crosswise into ¼-inch-thick slices).

3 In large bowl, toss potatoes, salt, pepper, and remaining 1 tablespoon oil until evenly coated.

4 Divide potatoes between prepared cookie sheets, spreading each batch into an even layer. Bake 25 minutes or until tender and crisp, turning potatoes over once and switching pans between upper and lower racks halfway through cooking.

EACH SERVING: ABOUT 173 CALORIES, 3G PROTEIN, 29G CARBOHYDRATE, 5G TOTAL FAT (1G SATURATED), 3G FIBER, 0MG CHOLESTEROL, 450MG SODIUM.

Lemony
OVEN FRIES

Prepare Classic Oven Fries, but in step 3, mix **1 teaspoon grated lemon peel, 2 tablespoons fresh lemon juice, 1 tablespoon dried oregano,** and **1 large clove garlic**, crushed with garlic press, with salt, pepper, and oil in bowl. Add potatoes and toss to coat. Complete recipe as in step 4.

Spicy
OVEN FRIES

Prepare Classic Oven Fries, but in step 3, mix **1 teaspoon onion powder, ½ teaspoon turmeric,** and **¼ teaspoon cayenne (ground red) pepper** with salt, pepper, and oil in bowl. Add potatoes and toss to coat. Complete recipe as in step 4.

BLT BURGERS

Dynamite grilled patties + bacon, lettuce, and tomato +
our "secret sauce" = burger bliss.

ACTIVE TIME: 15 MINUTES   TOTAL TIME: 25 MINUTES
MAKES: 4 BURGERS

¼   **cup ketchup**

¼   **cup light mayonnaise**

1   **tablespoon yellow mustard**

1¼   **pounds ground beef chuck**

8   **slices bacon**

4   **sesame-seed buns, split and toasted**

**sliced sweet onion, tomato, and romaine
   lettuce leaves**

1 Prepare outdoor grill for direct grilling over
medium heat.

2 In bowl, stir together ketchup, mayonnaise,
and mustard until blended. Makes about ½ cup.

3 Shape ground beef into 4 equal patties, each
about ¾-inch thick, handling meat as little as
possible. Crisscross each patty with 2 strips
bacon. Place, seam side down, on large plate.

4 Place patties on hot grill rack; cook 10 to 12
minutes for medium, or until desired doneness is
reached, turning over once.

5 Serve burgers on buns with onion, tomato,
lettuce, and sauce.

EACH SERVING: ABOUT 575 CALORIES, 34G PROTEIN,
27G CARBOHYDRATE, 36G TOTAL FAT (12G SATURATED),
2G FIBER, 111MG CHOLESTEROL, 870MG SODIUM.

TIP

For these burgers, opt for center-cut
bacon. It has a higher meat-to-fat ratio
than the less expensive varieties.

Gingered Burgers
WITH LIME SLAW

These spicy burgers are jazzed up with fresh ginger, cilantro, green onions, sesame oil, and crushed red pepper. A creamy lime slaw deliciously tames the heat.

ACTIVE TIME: 15 MINUTES   TOTAL TIME: 25 MINUTES
MAKES: 4 BURGERS

¼ cup light mayonnaise

1 tablespoon reduced-sodium soy sauce

2 limes

3½ cups (half of 16-ounce bag) shredded cabbage for coleslaw

½ teaspoon salt

1¼ pounds lean (90%) ground beef

½ cup loosely packed fresh cilantro leaves, coarsely chopped

2 green onions, chopped

1 tablespoon finely chopped, peeled fresh ginger

1 teaspoon Asian sesame oil

¼ teaspoon crushed red pepper

4 sesame-seed hamburger buns, split and toasted

1 **For Lime Slaw:** In cup, stir together mayonnaise and soy sauce until blended; set aside. From limes, grate ½ teaspoon peel and squeeze 3 tablespoons juice. In large bowl, toss together lime peel and juice with cabbage and ¼ teaspoon salt; set aside.

2 Lightly spray ridged grill pan or skillet with nonstick cooking spray and heat over medium heat until hot.

3 Meanwhile, in medium bowl, combine ground beef, cilantro, green onions, ginger, sesame oil, crushed red pepper, and remaining ¼ teaspoon salt until blended, but do not overmix. Shape beef mixture into 4 equal patties, each about ¾-inch thick, handling meat as little as possible.

4 Place patties in hot grill pan; cook 10 to 12 minutes for medium, or until desired doneness is reached, turning over once.

5 Place burgers on buns and top with slaw and soy mayonnaise. Serve with any additional slaw on the side.

....

EACH SERVING: ABOUT 430 CALORIES, 32G PROTEIN, 28G CARBOHYDRATE, 21G TOTAL FAT (7G SATURATED), 3G FIBER, 92MG CHOLESTEROL, 865MG SODIUM.

TIP

You'll need about a 1-inch piece of peeled fresh ginger for this recipe.

Meatloaf Burgers
WITH SAUTÉED CARROTS

We make meatloaf fun by serving it burger-style.
A simple side of sautéed carrots makes it kid-friendly, too.

ACTIVE TIME: 15 MINUTES   **TOTAL TIME:** 35 MINUTES
MAKES: 4 BURGERS

1   tablespoon butter or margarine

1   bag (16 ounces) baby carrots

½   teaspoon salt

¼   teaspoon ground black pepper

1   tablespoon brown sugar

¼   cup ketchup

1   tablespoon spicy brown mustard

1¼   pounds lean (90%) ground beef

1   stalk celery, finely chopped

½   small onion, finely chopped

¼   cup plain dried breadcrumbs

1   clove garlic, crushed with garlic press

2   teaspoons Worcestershire sauce

4   potato rolls, split and toasted

4   lettuce leaves

1 **For Sauteed Carrots:** In 12-inch skillet, heat *½ cup water* and butter over medium heat until simmering. Add carrots, ¼ teaspoon salt, and pepper; cook, covered, until carrots are tender, about 10 minutes. Uncover; stir in brown sugar and cook until carrots are coated and liquid evaporates, about 3 minutes longer. Remove pan from heat; cover and keep warm.

2 Meanwhile, lightly spray ridged grill pan or skillet with nonstick cooking spray and heat over medium heat until hot.

3 In cup, stir together ketchup and mustard until blended. In large bowl, combine 1 tablespoon ketchup mixture with ground beef, celery, onion, breadcrumbs, garlic, Worcestershire, and remaining ¼ teaspoon salt until blended, but do not overmix. Shape beef mixture into 4 equal patties, each about ¾-inch thick, handling meat as little as possible.

4 Place patties in hot grill pan; cook 10 to 12 minutes for medium, or until desired doneness is reached, turning over once.

5 Place burgers on rolls and top with lettuce and remaining ketchup mixture. Serve with carrots.

EACH SERVING: ABOUT 505 CALORIES, 36G PROTEIN, 52G CARBOHYDRATE, 18G TOTAL FAT (5G SATURATED), 6G FIBER, 87MG CHOLESTEROL, 975MG SODIUM.

Dressed to Kill

Looking for more burgers? Add pizzazz to Our Best Burger (page 14) with these tempting fixings and different breads.

- Prepared tapenade with olive oil mayonnaise, roasted red and yellow peppers, and sliced Italian bread

- Melted sharp Cheddar cheese, sliced pickles, and a sourdough roll

- Store-bought barbecue sauce*, potato roll, and corn relish

- Teriyaki sauce*, prepared horseradish, sliced green onion, and a toasted sourdough English muffin

- Fresh mozzarella, tomato, fresh basil leaves, and focaccia bread

- Sliced beets and onions, dilled sour cream, and pumpernickel bread

- Mango chutney, apple slices, plain Greek yogurt, and a pita

- Worcestershire sauce*, baby lettuce, blue cheese, and sliced French bread

- Melted pepper Jack cheese, tomato, avocado, cilantro, and a whole wheat tortilla

- Ketchup; pinch grated, peeled fresh ginger; sliced red onion; and a sesame-seed bun

- Honey mustard*, grilled peaches or nectarines, and whole-grain bread

*Brushed on during cooking

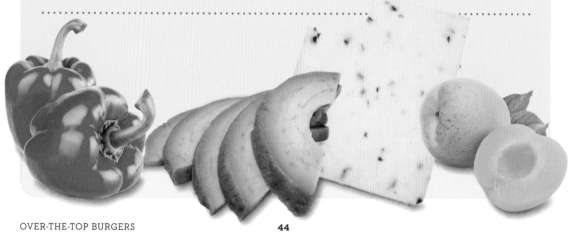

Southwest Sirloin
BURGERS

Everyone will flip for these super-juicy burgers
piled high with zesty chile-lime mayo, crunchy radishes,
and salsa on buttery toasted brioche buns.

ACTIVE TIME: 15 MINUTES **TOTAL TIME:** 21 MINUTES
MAKES: 4 BURGERS

¼ cup light mayonnaise

2 green onions, finely chopped

2 tablespoons canned, chopped mild green chiles, drained

1 teaspoon grated lime peel

1 teaspoon lime juice

salt

ground black pepper

5 radishes, thinly sliced

1¼ pounds lean (85%) ground beef sirloin

4 brioche hamburger buns, toasted

4 Boston lettuce leaves

¼ cup salsa

1 Prepare outdoor grill for covered direct grilling over medium heat.

2 In small bowl, stir together mayonnaise, green onions, chiles, lime peel, lime juice, ⅛ teaspoon salt, and ⅛ teaspoon pepper; set aside.

3 In strainer set over medium bowl, toss together radishes and ⅛ teaspoon salt; set aside.

4 Shape ground beef into 4 equal patties, each ¾-inch thick, handling meat as little as possible. Sprinkle ¼ teaspoon salt and ¼ teaspoon pepper on both sides of patties.

5 Place patties on hot grill rack; cook, covered, 7 minutes for medium, or until desired doneness is reached, turning over once.

6 Serve burgers on buns with lime mayonnaise, radishes, lettuce, and salsa.

EACH SERVING: ABOUT 415 CALORIES, 24G PROTEIN, 24G CARBOHYDRATE, 22G TOTAL FAT (7G SATURATED), 1G FIBER, 92MG CHOLESTEROL, 685MG SODIUM.

OVER-THE-TOP BURGERS

Greek Lamb
BURGERS

Cumin-scented burgers are topped with
a refreshing yogurt and mint sauce. Chopped walnuts
add a subtle nutty taste and pleasant crunch.

ACTIVE TIME: 20 MINUTES   TOTAL TIME: 30 MINUTES
MAKES: 4 BURGERS

YOGURT SAUCE

- 1   plum tomato, chopped
- ¼   cup plain low-fat yogurt
- 2   tablespoons light mayonnaise
- ¾   cup loosely packed fresh mint leaves, coarsely chopped
- ¼   teaspoon salt
- ¼   teaspoon ground black pepper

LAMB BURGERS

- 1¼ pounds ground lamb
- ¼   cup walnuts, chopped (optional)
- 1   clove garlic, crushed with garlic press
- 2   teaspoons ground cumin
- ¾   teaspoon salt
- 4   (6-inch) pitas
- 1   medium Kirby (pickling) cucumber, unpeeled and sliced

1 Prepare outdoor grill for direct grilling over medium heat.

2 **Prepare Yogurt Sauce:** In small bowl, stir together tomato, yogurt, mayonnaise, 2 tablespoons mint, and salt until blended; set aside. Makes about ¾ cup.

3 **Prepare Lamb Burgers:** In medium bowl, combine ground lamb, walnuts (if using), garlic, cumin, salt, and remaining mint until blended, but do not overmix. Shape lamb mixture into 4 equal patties, each about ¾-inch thick, handling meat as little as possible.

4 Place patties on hot grill rack; cook 10 to 12 minutes for medium, or until desired doneness is reached, turning over once.

5 To serve, cut off one-third from a side of each pita; save for making crumbs another day. Place burgers in pitas with yogurt sauce and cucumber.

EACH SERVING: ABOUT 485 CALORIES, 32G PROTEIN, 31G CARBOHYDRATE, 25G TOTAL FAT (10G SATURATED), 3G FIBER, 105MG CHOLESTEROL, 985MG SODIUM.

Chicken Apple Burgers
(page 56)

3 | Wing It Burgers

Truth be told, chicken and turkey burgers have a bit of an image problem. When compared to a juicy beef burger, too often they get a bad rap for being dry and tasteless.

But it doesn't have to be that way. Fat adds flavor, and because ground poultry is leaner than ground beef, it requires a bit more TLC. For our Herb Burgers (page 51), we bolster the taste with stir-ins like fresh dill, dried mint, and grated onion. Fat also adds moisture, so to compensate, we add extra liquid (such as chili sauce, molasses, cayenne pepper sauce, and Worcestershire sauce) to our Barbecue Burgers (page 51), and mix in water-packed veggies like zucchini for our Texas Chicken Burgers (page 54).

The final cooks' challenge when crafting a great poultry burger? It must be thoroughly cooked. Eliminate the guesswork and use an instant-read thermometer to test for doneness. Cook chicken and turkey burgers to 165°F—no higher—and your burgers will stay moist inside.

Chicken
BURGERS

If you're hankering for a plain, straightforward burger,
this one's for you. Season the patties with crunchy kosher salt
and freshly ground black pepper before grilling,
and you're good to go.

ACTIVE TIME: 20 MINUTES   **TOTAL TIME:** 32 MINUTES
MAKES: 4 BURGERS

1   pound ground chicken breast

1   medium carrot, grated (½ cup)

2   green onions, minced

1   clove garlic, crushed with garlic press

4   hamburger buns, split and warmed

sliced cucumber, lettuce leaves, and
    green onion (optional)

1 Prepare outdoor grill for direct grilling over medium heat.

2 In medium bowl, combine ground chicken, carrot, green onions, and garlic until blended, but do not overmix.

3 On waxed paper, shape chicken mixture into four 3½-inch round patties, handling mixture as little as possible (mixture will be very soft and moist). Spray both sides of patties with nonstick cooking spray.

4 Place patties on hot grill rack; cook about 12 minutes or just until chicken loses its pink color throughout, turning once.

5 Serve burgers on warmed buns with cucumber slices, lettuce leaves, and green onion, if using.

EACH SERVING: ABOUT 275 CALORIES, 30G PROTEIN, 24G CARBOHYDRATE, 5G TOTAL FAT (1G SATURATED), 2G FIBER, 72MG CHOLESTEROL, 310MG SODIUM.

TIP

Chicken patties are delicate, so if you have a grill with widely spaced grates, we recommend placing the burgers on a perforated grill topper to keep them intact.

More CHICKEN BURGERS!

It's a cinch to jazz up our Chicken Burgers (left)
to please any craving, so take your pick
from a favorite flavor family—herb, barbecue, or teriyaki.

Herb
BURGERS

Prepare and cook Chicken Burgers, but in step
2, add **2 tablespoons finely chopped fresh
dill, 1 tablespoon dried mint, 1 tablespoon
fresh lemon juice, 1 teaspoon ground cumin,
½ teaspoon salt,** and ⅛ **teaspoon cayenne
(ground red) pepper** to ground chicken mixture.

EACH SERVING: ABOUT 280 CALORIES, 31G PROTEIN,
25G CARBOHYDRATE, 5G TOTAL FAT (1G SATURATED),
2G FIBER, 72MG CHOLESTEROL, 605MG SODIUM.

Barbecue
BURGERS

Prepare and cook Chicken Burgers, but in step
2, add **2 tablespoons chili sauce, 1 tablespoon
light (mild) molasses, 2 teaspoons cayenne
pepper sauce, 2 teaspoons Worcestershire
sauce,** and ¼ **teaspoon salt** to ground chicken
mixture.

EACH SERVING: ABOUT 295 CALORIES, 31G PROTEIN,
30G CARBOHYDRATE, 5G TOTAL FAT (1G SATURATED),
2G FIBER, 72MG CHOLESTEROL, 715MG SODIUM.

Teriyaki
BURGERS

Prepare and cook Chicken Burgers, but in step
2, add **2 tablespoons soy sauce, 1 tablespoon
seasoned rice vinegar, 2 teaspoons grated,
peeled fresh ginger,** and **2 teaspoons Asian
sesame oil** to ground chicken mixture.

EACH SERVING: ABOUT 305 CALORIES, 31G PROTEIN,
26G CARBOHYDRATE, 8G TOTAL FAT (2G SATURATED),
2G FIBER, 72MG CHOLESTEROL, 940MG SODIUM.

TIP

Prepare the teriyaki burgers just before
cooking to prevent the ginger from changing
the texture of the ground chicken.

Jerk Chicken
BURGERS

These Jamaican-spiced burgers are topped
with a fabulous mango-yogurt sauce.

ACTIVE TIME: 20 MINUTES   **TOTAL TIME:** 30 MINUTES
MAKES: 4 BURGERS

5   green onions

1   pound ground chicken or turkey

2   teaspoons Jamaican jerk seasoning

½   teaspoon salt

2   tablespoons vegetable oil

½   cup plain Greek yogurt

1   mango, peeled and chopped

4   hamburger buns, split and toasted

Bibb lettuce leaves

1   Finely chop 3 green onions. In large bowl, combine chopped green onions, ground chicken, jerk seasoning, and salt until blended, but do not overmix. Shape chicken mixture into 4 equal patties, each about ½-inch thick, handling mixture as little as possible.

2   In 12-inch skillet, heat oil over medium-high heat until hot. Add patties and cook about 10 minutes or just until chicken loses its pink color throughout, turning over once.

3   Meanwhile, chop remaining 2 green onions. In small bowl, mix yogurt, chopped green onions, and mango.

4   Serve burgers on buns and top with lettuce and mango-yogurt sauce.

EACH SERVING: ABOUT 406 CALORIES, 27G PROTEIN, 37G CARBOHYDRATE, 18G TOTAL FAT (6G SATURATED), 3G FIBER, 96MG CHOLESTEROL, 717MG SODIUM.

TIP

To pick a ripe mango, always judge by feel—not by the red color that appears on some varieties. Gently squeeze the fruit. If it gives slightly, it's ripe.

Texas Chicken
BURGERS

These juicy chili-spiked burgers do the Texas two-step
served with a side of speedy baked beans.

ACTIVE TIME: 15 MINUTES   TOTAL TIME: 25 MINUTES
MAKES: 4 BURGERS

1   pound ground chicken

2   green onions, chopped

1   small zucchini (about 5 ounces), grated

1   medium carrot, grated

1   tablespoon chili powder

3/4 teaspoon salt

1/4 teaspoon ground cumin

1/8 teaspoon cayenne (ground red) pepper

1   can (16 ounces) vegetarian baked beans

1   tablespoon Dijon mustard

1   tablespoon light (mild) molasses

2   teaspoons vegetable oil

4   whole-grain sandwich rolls

lettuce leaves

1 In medium bowl, combine ground chicken, green onions, zucchini, carrot, chili powder, salt, cumin, and cayenne pepper until blended, but do not overmix.

2 On waxed paper, shape chicken mixture into four 3½-inch round patties, handling mixture as little as possible. Set aside.

3 In 1-quart saucepan over medium heat, bring beans, mustard, and molasses to a boil.

4 Meanwhile, in 12-inch skillet, heat oil over medium-high heat until hot. Add patties; cook about 10 minutes or just until chicken loses its pink color throughout, turning once. Place lettuce on sandwich rolls and top with burger. Serve with baked beans.

EACH SERVING: ABOUT 487 CALORIES, 34G PROTEIN, 58G CARBOHYDRATE, 15G TOTAL FAT (4G SATURATED), 11G FIBER, 91MG CHOLESTEROL, 1,317MG SODIUM.

TIP

Use a flexible spatula to place the delicate patties in the hot skillet and turn them over while cooking.

Chicken Apple
BURGERS

Ground chicken breast is very lean, so we added
grated apple to these burgers for extra moisture.
The jarred cranberry sauce topping adds another layer
of juiciness and flavor. For photo, see page 48.

ACTIVE TIME: 15 MINUTES   **TOTAL TIME:** 25 MINUTES
MAKES: 4 BURGERS

2   Granny Smith apples, cored

½   teaspoon poultry seasoning

½   teaspoon salt

¼   teaspoon ground black pepper

1   pound ground chicken

¼   cup finely chopped celery (about ½ stalk)

4   hamburger buns, split

½   cup whole-berry cranberry sauce

1 From each apple, cut 6 thin slices crosswise from center (for a total of 12 apple rings). From remainder, coarsely shred ¾ cup apples.

2 Spray ridged grill pan or skillet with nonstick cooking spray and heat over medium-high heat until hot.

3 Meanwhile, in medium bowl, stir together shredded apple with poultry seasoning, salt, and pepper until blended. Mix in ground chicken and celery until blended, but do not overmix. Shape chicken mixture into 4 equal patties, each about ½-inch thick, handling mixture as little as possible.

4 Place patties in hot grill pan; cook 10 to 12 minutes or just until chicken loses its pink color throughout, turning over once. Serve burgers on buns and top with with apple rings and cranberry sauce.

EACH SERVING: ABOUT 385 CALORIES, 24G PROTEIN, 47G CARBOHYDRATE, 12G TOTAL FAT (1G SATURATED), 4G FIBER, 0MG CHOLESTEROL, 610MG SODIUM.

Chicken Burgers
WITH BLACK BEAN SALSA

Olé! You'll love these Mexi-burgers
served on toasted tortillas
with a zesty bean, avocado, and corn salsa.

ACTIVE TIME: 20 MINUTES **TOTAL TIME:** 45 MINUTES
MAKES: 4 BURGERS

- ½ small red onion
- 2 tablespoons olive oil
- 1 medium carrot, finely chopped
- 1 medium celery stalk, finely chopped
- 2 tablespoons fresh lime juice
- ¾ teaspoon salt
- ½ teaspoon coarsely ground black pepper
- 1 large tomato, seeded and diced
- 1 ripe avocado, diced
- 1 can (15 to 16 ounces) black beans, rinsed and drained
- 1 can (8¼ ounces) whole-kernel corn, drained
- 1 pound ground chicken
- 1 slice white bread, torn into coarse crumbs
- 1 can (4 ounces) chopped mild green chiles, drained
- 4 (8-inch) flour tortillas
- 1 small head Boston or romaine lettuce

1 Mince onion; reserve 1 tablespoon for black bean salsa.

2 In 12-inch nonstick skillet, heat 1 tablespoon oil over medium heat until hot. Add carrot, celery, and remaining onion and cook until very tender, about 10 minutes.

3 Prepare Black Bean Salsa: In small bowl, mix together lime juice, ¼ teaspoon salt, and pepper. Stir in tomato, avocado, beans, corn, and reserved onion. Set aside.

4 In large bowl, combine cooked vegetable mixture, ground chicken, breadcrumbs, chiles, and remaining ½ teaspoon salt until blended, but do not overmix. Shape chicken mixture into 4 equal patties, each about ¾-inch thick, handling mixture as little as possible.

5 In same skillet, heat remaining 1 tablespoon oil over medium heat until hot. Add patties and cook about 10 minutes or just until chicken loses its pink color throughout, turning over once.

6 Meanwhile, arrange oven rack 4 inches from heat source. Preheat broiler. Place tortillas on cookie sheet and broil until lightly toasted, turning once.

7 To serve, place 1 tortilla on each of 4 plates. Top each tortilla with a few lettuce leaves and 1 burger. Spoon salsa evenly over burgers.

EACH SERVING: ABOUT 601 CALORIES, 33G PROTEIN, 63G CARBOHYDRATE, 27G TOTAL FAT (6G SATURATED), 14G FIBER, 91MG CHOLESTEROL, 1,559MG SODIUM.

Grilled Turkey
BURGERS

Cajun seasoning and hot pepper sauce
give these burgers heat, while grated zucchini
lends moisture and a touch of sweetness.

ACTIVE TIME: 15 MINUTES   **TOTAL TIME:** 25 MINUTES
MAKES: 4 BURGERS

- 1   medium zucchini (6 ounces), shredded
- 2   tablespoons grated onion
- 1   teaspoon Cajun seasoning
- 1   pound ground turkey breast
- 4   ears corn, husks and silk removed
- ¼   cup ketchup
- ½   teaspoon hot pepper sauce
- 4   whole wheat hamburger buns, split and toasted
- 4   Boston lettuce leaves
- 1   small tomato, sliced

pickle spears (optional)

1   Prepare outdoor grill for covered direct grilling over medium heat.

2   In medium bowl, combine zucchini, onion, and Cajun seasoning until blended. Mix in ground turkey until blended, but do not overmix. Shape turkey mixture into 4 equal patties, each about ¾-inch thick, handling mixture as little as possible. Spray both sides of patties with nonstick cooking spray.

3   Place patties on hot grill rack; cook 12 to 14 minutes or just until turkey loses its pink color throughout, turning over once.

4   After burgers have cooked 2 minutes, add corn to grill rack. Cover and cook 10 to 12 minutes or until corn is browned in spots, turning occasionally.

5   Meanwhile, in small bowl, combine ketchup and hot sauce; set aside.

6   Place burgers on buns and top with lettuce, tomato, and sauce. Serve with corn and pickle spears, if using.

....

EACH SERVING: ABOUT 350 CALORIES, 35G PROTEIN, 27G CARBOHYDRATE, 13G TOTAL FAT (3G SATURATED), 3G FIBER, 106MG CHOLESTEROL, 615MG SODIUM.

Hoisin
TURKEY BURGERS

Ground poultry lends itself well to Asian flavors,
and these gingery burgers topped with sweet and spicy
hoisin sauce couldn't be easier to slap on the grill.

ACTIVE TIME: 10 MINUTES **TOTAL TIME:** 22 MINUTES
MAKES: 4 BURGERS

1   pound ground turkey

¼   cup chopped fresh cilantro

2   green onions, finely chopped

2   tablespoons reduced-sodium soy sauce

1   tablespoon minced, peeled fresh ginger

½   teaspoon salt

¼   teaspoon ground black pepper

4   hamburger buns, split and toasted

¼   cup hoisin sauce

1 In medium bowl, combine ground turkey, cilantro, green onions, soy sauce, ginger, salt, and pepper until blended, but do not overmix. Shape turkey mixture into 4 equal patties, each about ¾-inch thick, handling mixture as little as possible.

2 Lightly spray 12-inch nonstick skillet with cooking spray and heat over medium heat until hot. Add patties and cook 12 to 14 minutes or just until turkey loses its pink color throughout, turning over once.

3 Place burgers on buns and top with hoisin sauce.

EACH SERVING: ABOUT 329 CALORIES, 28G PROTEIN, 30G CARBOHYDRATE, 11G TOTAL FAT (3G SATURATED), 2G FIBER, 76MG CHOLESTEROL, 1,100MG SODIUM.

Bacon & Tomato
TURKEY BURGERS

Burger, meet leftover roast turkey!
Studded with bacon and veggies, this recipe is equally fabulous
with rotisserie chicken from the supermarket.

ACTIVE TIME: 20 MINUTES   **TOTAL TIME:** 30 MINUTES
MAKES: 6 BURGERS

6   slices bacon, diced

5   slices white bread

2   cups finely minced cooked turkey
    (about ¾ pound)

2   medium celery stalks, minced

1   small onion, grated

2   large eggs

¼   teaspoon salt

⅛   teaspoon ground black pepper

3   tablespoons butter or margarine

6   Kaiser rolls, split

lettuce leaves, for topping

1   medium tomato, thinly sliced

1 In 12-inch skillet over medium-low heat, cook bacon until browned; remove to paper towels to drain. Pour off all drippings from skillet, wipe skillet clean with paper towels, and set aside.

2 In large bowl, tear 4 bread slices into small pieces. Add turkey, celery, onion, eggs, salt, pepper, and bacon; mix well. Shape turkey mixture into six 3-inch patties.

3 On waxed paper, tear remaining bread slice into fine crumbs. Using hands, press crumbs into patties to coat completely.

4 In same skillet, melt butter over medium-high heat. Add patties and cook about 10 minutes or until lightly browned.

5 Place burgers on rolls and top with lettuce and tomato.

EACH SERVING: ABOUT 441 CALORIES, 29G PROTEIN, 42G CARBOHYDRATE, 16G TOTAL FAT (7G SATURATED), 2G FIBER, 143MG CHOLESTEROL, 793MG SODIUM.

Turkey Burgers
WITH SWEET POTATO FRIES

Don't be fooled—this healthy burger-and-fries combo
only tastes indulgent.

ACTIVE TIME: 20 MINUTES   TOTAL TIME: 40 MINUTES
MAKES: 4 BURGERS

SWEET POTATO FRIES

2   small sweet potatoes (1 pound)

2   tablespoons olive oil

1   teaspoon chili powder

¼   teaspoon salt

BURGERS

1   pound ground turkey breast

2   cloves garlic, crushed with garlic press

½   cup chopped fresh cilantro

1   teaspoon chili powder

¼   teaspoon salt

½   ripe avocado

2   teaspoons fresh lime juice

4   whole-grain sandwich thins, split and toasted

sliced tomato, sliced cucumber, lettuce leaves,
   and sprouts (optional)

1 Prepare Sweet Potato Fries: Preheat oven
to 450°F. Cut unpeeled potatoes lengthwise into
¼-inch-wide sticks. On large rimmed baking
sheet, toss potatoes with oil, chili powder, and
salt. Roast potatoes 20 to 25 minutes or until
crisp, shaking pan once halfway through cooking.

2 Prepare Burgers: Meanwhile, prepare
outdoor grill for direct grilling over medium heat.

3 In medium bowl, combine ground turkey,
garlic, cilantro, chili powder, and salt. Shape
turkey mixture into 4 patties, handling mixture
as little as possible. Spray both sides of patties
with nonstick cooking spray.

4 Place patties on hot grill rack; cook 12 to 15
minutes or just until turkey loses its pink color
throughout, turning once.

5 While burgers are cooking, in small bowl,
mash avocado with lime juice.

6 Place burgers on sandwich thins and top with
tomato and cucumber slices, lettuce leaves, and
sprouts, if using. Serve with fries.

....

EACH SERVING: ABOUT 470 CALORIES, 30G PROTEIN,
46G CARBOHYDRATE, 21G TOTAL FAT (4G SATURATED),
11G FIBER, 72MG CHOLESTEROL, 640MG SODIUM.

TIP

For a super-deluxe burger, prepare the
recipe as directed, but in step 3 swap in
parsley for the cilantro. Omit the avocado
mixture. Slather the grilled burgers with
mayo, top with crumbled blue cheese
and cooked bacon, and serve on toasted
ciabatta buns with baby spinach.

TURKEY BURGER
Deluxe

These zesty burgers get the deluxe treatment
with apple and horseradish and are served with a side
of tangy coleslaw and DIY pita chips.

ACTIVE TIME: 30 MINUTES   **TOTAL TIME:** 39 MINUTES
MAKES: 6 BURGERS

TANGY COLESLAW

- ½ cup plain low-fat yogurt
- 2 tablespoons white wine vinegar
- 1 teaspoon dried mustard
- 1 teaspoon sugar
- ½ teaspoon salt
- ¼ small head green cabbage, thinly sliced (about 2 cups)
- 1 medium carrot, shredded
- 1 medium red pepper, cut into 1-inch-long matchstick-thin strips

BURGERS

- 1 pound ground turkey
- 2 tablespoons prepared white horseradish, drained
- 1 medium Granny Smith apple, peeled and shredded
- ½ small onion, grated
- 4 teaspoons finely chopped fresh parsley
- 1 (6-inch) pita
- 1 tablespoon butter or margarine, softened

1 Prepare Tangy Coleslaw: In medium bowl, whisk together yogurt, vinegar, mustard, sugar, and salt until blended. Stir in cabbage, carrot, and red pepper; set aside.

2 Arrange oven rack 4 inches from heat source. Spray broiler rack with nonstick cooking spray. Preheat broiler.

3 Prepare Burgers: In medium bowl, combine ground turkey, horseradish, apple, onion, and 3 teaspoons parsley until blended, but do not overmix. Shape turkey mixture into 6 equal patties, each about 1-inch thick, handling mixture as little as possible.

4 Place patties on prepared broiler rack; broil burgers 9 to 10 minutes or just until turkey loses its pink color throughout, turning over once.

5 Meanwhile, split pita horizontally in half; cut each half into quarters. In cup, mix butter and remaining 1 teaspoon parsley; spread on cut sides of pita triangles. Place triangles on cookie sheet; broil 1 to 2 minutes or until golden.

6 Place burgers on 6 plates and serve with coleslaw and pita chips.

EACH SERVING: ABOUT 207 CALORIES, 18G PROTEIN, 16G CARBOHYDRATE, 8G TOTAL FAT (3G SATURATED), 2G FIBER, 57MG CHOLESTEROL, 353MG SODIUM.

TURKEY BURGERS
in Lettuce Cups

These springtime burgers get their crunch from a tasty radish-pickle relish. Serve on tender Boston or Bibb lettuce leaves—you won't even miss the bun.

ACTIVE TIME: 25 MINUTES   TOTAL TIME: 35 MINUTES
MAKES: 4 BURGERS

½ cup radishes, minced

⅓ cup dill pickles, minced

1 hard-cooked egg, minced

⅓ cup light mayonnaise

3 tablespoons ketchup

1 tablespoon Dijon mustard

⅛ teaspoon sugar

1 pound ground turkey

1 tablespoon vegetable oil

lettuce leaves, for serving

1 small tomato, sliced

1 medium cucumber, thinly sliced

1 In small bowl, mix radishes, pickles, and egg with fork; set aside.

2 In another small bowl, whisk together mayonnaise, ketchup, mustard, and sugar until blended.

3 In medium bowl, combine ground turkey and 2 tablespoons mayonnaise mixture until blended, but do not overmix. Shape turkey mixture into 4 equal patties, each about ¾-inch thick, handling mixture as little as possible.

4 Heat oil in 10-inch nonstick skillet over medium-high heat until hot. Add patties and cook about 10 minutes or just until turkey loses its pink color throughout, turning over once.

5 To serve, line 4 plates with lettuce leaves. Spoon half of relish onto lettuce; place 1 burger on top. Top burgers with tomato, cucumber, remaining mayonnaise mixture, and remaining relish.

EACH SERVING: ABOUT 304 CALORIES, 25G PROTEIN, 10G CARBOHYDRATE, 18G TOTAL FAT (4G SATURATED), 2G FIBER, 129MG CHOLESTEROL, 515MG SODIUM.

Sesame
TURKEY BURGERS

Dark Asian sesame oil and toasted sesame-seed buns
give these burgers a terrific nutty taste.

ACTIVE TIME: 15 MINUTES   TOTAL TIME: 25 MINUTES
MAKES: 4 BURGERS

¼ cup light mayonnaise

1 tablespoon soy sauce

1¼ pounds ground turkey or chicken

½ cup loosely packed fresh cilantro leaves, coarsely chopped

3 green onions, chopped

1 tablespoon dry sherry

1 tablespoon finely chopped peeled, fresh ginger

1 teaspoon Asian sesame oil

¾ teaspoon salt

¼ teaspoon crushed red pepper

4 sesame-seed buns, split and toasted

1 Prepare outdoor grill for direct grilling over medium heat.

2 In cup, stir together mayonnaise and soy sauce until blended; set aside. Makes about ¼ cup.

3 In medium bowl, combine ground turkey, cilantro, green onions, sherry, ginger, sesame oil, salt, and crushed red pepper until blended, but do not overmix. Shape turkey mixture into 4 equal patties, each about ¾-inch thick. Spray both sides of patties with nonstick cooking spray.

4 Place patties on hot grill rack; cook 12 to 14 minutes or just until turkey loses its pink color throughout, turning over once. Serve burgers on buns with soy mayonnaise.

....

EACH SERVING: ABOUT 406 CALORIES, 34G PROTEIN, 25G CARBOHYDRATE, 20G TOTAL FAT (5G SATURATED), 1G FIBER, 100MG CHOLESTEROL, 1,053MG SODIUM.

Chipotle Nacho Burgers
(page 73)

4 | Cheesy Burgers

Oozy, melty, and dripping with flavor, it's no wonder the cheeseburger has top-tier status in the pantheon of best-ever burgers. And while processed squares (such as sliced American cheese) have their fan base, if you're truly serious about your burger, you owe it to yourself to experiment with other melt-friendly options. Try our Burgers with French Onions (page 71) with Gruyère cheese, New England-Style Cheeseburgers (page 77) with sharp Cheddar cheese, or Blue & Black Burgers (page 72) stuffed with—you guessed it—tangy blue cheese.

To get that melted effect on your char-grilled beauty, speed is everything. Place the cheese on the meat, cover, and start checking once a minute has passed.

BURGERS
with French Onions

Ooh la-la!
These burgers are topped with sautéed onions and mushrooms,
melted Gruyère cheese, and garlic mayonnaise.

ACTIVE TIME: 15 MINUTES   TOTAL TIME: 34 MINUTES
MAKES: 4 BURGERS

⅓ cup light mayonnaise

¼ cup loosely packed fresh parsley leaves, finely chopped

1 small clove garlic, crushed with garlic press

½ teaspoon ground black pepper

2 teaspoons olive oil

1 medium red onion (6 to 8 ounces), cut in half and thinly sliced

4 ounces mushrooms, sliced

1 teaspoon sugar

½ teaspoon salt

1¼ pounds lean (85%) ground beef

1 ounce Gruyère cheese, shredded (¼ cup)

4 brioche hamburger buns, toasted

4 Boston lettuce leaves

1 Prepare outdoor grill for covered direct grilling over medium heat.

2 In small bowl, stir together mayonnaise, parsley, garlic, and ¼ teaspoon pepper until blended; set aside.

3 In 12-inch skillet, heat oil over medium-high heat until hot. Add onion; cook, stirring occasionally, until it begins to soften, 3 to 4 minutes. Add mushrooms, *½ cup water*, sugar, and ¼ teaspoon salt; cover and cook, stirring occasionally, until mushrooms are tender, 5 to 6 minutes longer.

4 Meanwhile, shape ground beef into 4 equal patties, each ¾-inch thick, handling meat as little as possible. Sprinkle remaining ¼ teaspoon salt and ¼ teaspoon pepper on both sides of patties.

5 Place patties on hot grill rack; cook about 7 minutes for medium, or until desired doneness is reached, turning over once. Top each burger with ¼ cup onion mixture and 1 tablespoon cheese. Cover; cook until cheese has melted, about 1 minute longer. Serve burgers on buns with garlic mayonnaise and lettuce.

....

EACH SERVING: ABOUT 500 CALORIES, 34G PROTEIN, 33G CARBOHYDRATE, 33G TOTAL FAT (12G SATURATED), 2G FIBER, 197MG CHOLESTEROL, 880MG SODIUM.

Blue & Black
BURGERS

These char-grilled burgers have a tasty surprise inside:
luscious blue cheese. Brushing the buttery brioche buns with a basil-
infused oil before toasting makes this a summer winner.

ACTIVE TIME: 15 MINUTES   **TOTAL TIME:** 29 MINUTES
MAKES: 4 BURGERS

- 2 **tablespoons olive oil**
- 2 **tablespoons chopped fresh basil leaves**
- 4 **brioche hamburger buns, split**
- 1¼ **pounds ground beef chuck**
- 4 **ounces blue cheese, divided into four 1-inch chunks**
- ¾ **teaspoon salt**
- 1 **tablespoon coarsely ground black pepper**
- 4 **thin slices sweet onion**

1 Prepare outdoor grill for direct grilling over medium heat.

2 In cup, combine oil and basil; brush oil on 1 cut side of each bun. Set buns aside.

3 Hold one-fourth of ground beef in hand; press chunk of blue cheese into center, then lightly press meat around cheese to enclose completely. Patty will be about 1½ inches thick. Repeat with remaining ground beef and blue cheese. Sprinkle salt and pepper on both sides of patties.

4 Place patties on hot grill rack; cook 14 to 16 minutes for medium, or until desired doneness is reached, turning over once.

5 About 2 minutes before burgers are done, add buns, cut sides down, to grill rack. Grill just until toasted. Place burgers on buns and top with onion slices.

....

EACH SERVING: ABOUT 745 CALORIES, 40G PROTEIN, 39G CARBOHYDRATE, 47G TOTAL FAT (17G SATURATED), 2G FIBER, 190MG CHOLESTEROL, 1,235MG SODIUM.

TIP

For this recipe, choose a premium blue cheese like Stilton or Gorgonzola.

Chipotle Nacho BURGERS

Don't mistake ground chipotle chile pepper for chili powder (which is a blend of spices). Made from smoked jalapeños, chipotle pepper adds a blast of smoky heat to these sizzling burgers. For photo, see page 68.

ACTIVE TIME: 20 MINUTES   **TOTAL TIME:** 33 MINUTES
MAKES: 4 BURGERS

1¼ pounds lean (90%) ground beef

1½ teaspoons ground chipotle chile pepper

¼ teaspoon salt

4 slices Monterey Jack cheese (1 ounce each)

4 hamburger buns, split and toasted

1 cup mild or medium salsa

1 In large bowl, combine ground beef, chipotle pepper, and salt until blended, but do not overmix. Shape beef mixture into four 3½-inch patties, handling meat as little as possible.

2 Lightly spray ridged grill pan or 12-inch skillet with nonstick cooking spray and heat over medium heat until hot.

3 Place patties in hot grill pan. For medium, cook 6 minutes, and then turn burgers over to cook 3 minutes. Top each burger with 1 slice cheese; cook 2 to 3 minutes or until cheese melts.

4 Serve burgers on buns and top with salsa.

....

EACH SERVING: ABOUT 495 CALORIES, 40G PROTEIN, 26G CARBOHYDRATE, 24G TOTAL FAT (11G SATURATED), 4G FIBER, 121MG CHOLESTEROL, 830MG SODIUM.

Cheese Wiz
Cheeseburger mastery is as easy as 1-2-3!

1 Prep your cheese: Firm cheeses (Cheddar, Parmesan, Monterey Jack) should be sliced, shredded, or freshly grated; soft cheeses (goat, Feta, blue) should be crumbled.

2 Make sure the burgers are cooked through (or to your liking) before topping with cheese. If you add cheese too early, it will melt away and burn.

3 Give the cheese time to melt before serving. When grilling, cover the grill for about 1 minute after adding the cheese. For stovetop burgers, cover the pan. For crumbly cheeses, sprinkle them over your cooked burgers as soon as you take them off the heat (the cheese will soften by the time you serve the burgers).

INSIDE-OUT BURGERS
with Avocado & Sprouts

Stuffed with Cheddar cheese and topped
with citrusy mashed avocado and cilantro-spiked sprouts,
these lean beef burgers are absolutely decadent.

ACTIVE TIME: 20 MINUTES   TOTAL TIME: 32 MINUTES
MAKES: 4 BURGERS

1¼ **pounds lean (90%) ground beef**

2 **ounces shredded sharp Cheddar cheese (½ cup)**

1 **teaspoon salt**

¼ **teaspoon ground black pepper**

1 **ripe avocado**

1 **tablespoon fresh lime juice**

1 **cup alfalfa or radish sprouts**

¼ **cup loosely packed fresh cilantro leaves, chopped**

4 **whole-grain hamburger buns, split**

2 **small tomatoes, each cut into 4 wedges**

1 Shape ground beef into eight 3½-inch patties, handling meat as little as possible. Place Cheddar in center of 4 patties, leaving ½-inch border around each patty's edge. Top with remaining 4 patties, and press edges together to seal burgers well. Sprinkle ½ teaspoon salt and pepper on both sides of patties.

2 Lightly spray ridged grill pan with nonstick cooking spray and heat over medium heat until hot. Add burgers and cook 12 minutes for medium, or until desired doneness is reached, turning over once.

3 Meanwhile, in small bowl, mash avocado with lime juice and remaining ½ teaspoon salt. In another small bowl, combine alfalfa sprouts and cilantro.

4 Serve burgers on buns with sprout and avocado mixtures. Serve tomato wedges on the side.

EACH SERVING: ABOUT 480 CALORIES, 36G PROTEIN, 25G CARBOHYDRATE, 27G TOTAL FAT (9G SATURATED), 5G FIBER, 102MG CHOLESTEROL, 730MG SODIUM.

 TIP

Look for fresh-smelling sprouts that have been properly refrigerated, and always rinse thoroughly under cold running water before using.

Pimiento
CHEESEBURGERS

These Southern-inspired burgers are topped with the best pimiento cheese fixings: sharp Cheddar, mayo, diced pimientos, Worcestershire, and a dash of hot pepper sauce.

ACTIVE TIME: 10 MINUTES   TOTAL TIME: 18 MINUTES
MAKES: 4 BURGERS

1¼ pounds ground beef chuck

2 ounces sharp Cheddar cheese, shredded (½ cup)

¼ cup jarred diced pimientos, drained

2½ tablespoons light mayonnaise

1 tablespoon chopped green onion

¼ teaspoon hot pepper sauce

¼ teaspoon Worcestershire sauce

½ teaspoon coarsely ground black pepper

¾ teaspoon salt

4 hamburger buns, split

1 Divide ground beef into 4 mounds (about 5 ounces each), and loosely shape into balls.

2 Using your hands, gently flatten balls into ¾-inch-thick patties, handling meat as little as possible. Smooth patty edges with your fingers.

3 Place patties on a flat surface. Using your thumbs, press into centers of patties to make deep indentations. Refrigerate until ready to grill. In small bowl, mix Cheddar, pimientos, mayonnaise, green onion, hot pepper sauce, and Worcestershire sauce until blended; set aside.

4 Prepare outdoor grill for direct grilling over medium-high heat, or heat ridged grill pan over medium-high heat until very hot.

5 Place patties on hot grill rack. Cook 8 to 12 minutes for medium, or until desired doneness is reached, turning over once.

6 Place burgers on buns and top with pimiento mixture.

EACH SERVING: ABOUT 469 CALORIES, 32G PROTEIN, 23G CARBOHYDRATE, 26G TOTAL FAT (10G SATURATED), 1G FIBER, 101MG CHOLESTEROL, 882MG SODIUM.

New England-Style
CHEESEBURGERS

Tart green apples give these Cheddar burgers a regional spin. Serve with coarse grain mustard instead of the typical ketchup.

ACTIVE TIME: 10 MINUTES   **TOTAL TIME:** 19 MINUTES
MAKES: 4 BURGERS

1¼ pounds ground beef chuck

½ teaspoon coarsely ground black pepper

¾ teaspoon salt

4 slices sharp Cheddar cheese (1 ounce each)

4 hamburger buns, split

12 thin slices Granny Smith apple

12 thin slices red onion

1 Divide ground beef into 4 mounds (about 5 ounces each), and loosely shape into balls.

2 Using your hands, gently flatten balls into ¾-inch-thick patties, handling meat as little as possible. Smooth patty edges with your fingers.

3 Place patties on a flat surface. Using your thumbs, press into centers of patties to make deep indentations. Refrigerate until ready to grill.

4 Prepare outdoor grill for covered direct grilling over medium-high heat, or heat ridged grill pan over medium-high heat until very hot. Sprinkle salt and pepper on both sides of patties.

5 Place patties on hot grill rack. Cook 8 to 12 minutes for medium, or until desired doneness is reached, turning over once. Top each burger with 1 slice cheese. Cover and cook until cheese has melted, about 1 minute longer. Place burgers on buns and top with apple and onion slices.

EACH SERVING: ABOUT 494 CALORIES, 37G PROTEIN, 31G CARBOHYDRATE, 24G TOTAL FAT (10G SATURATED), 3G FIBER, 105MG CHOLESTEROL, 968MG SODIUM.

Tapas BURGERS

These tasty burgers get their Spanish flair
from a creamy roasted pepper sauce and manchego cheese.

ACTIVE TIME: 10 MINUTES   **TOTAL TIME:** 18 MINUTES

MAKES: 4 BURGERS

1¼ **pounds ground beef chuck**

½ **teaspoon coarsely ground black pepper**

¾ **teaspoon salt**

1 **cup jarred roasted red peppers, drained and patted dry**

¼ **cup light mayonnaise**

4 **ounces manchego cheese, shredded (1 cup)**

4 **hamburger buns, split**

1 Divide ground beef into 4 mounds (about 5 ounces each), and loosely shape into balls.

2 Using your hands, gently flatten balls into ¾-inch-thick patties, handling meat as little as possible. Smooth patty edges with your fingers.

3 Place patties on a flat surface. Using your thumbs, press into centers of patties to make deep indentations. Refrigerate until ready to grill.

4 Prepare outdoor grill for direct grilling over medium-high heat, or heat ridged grill pan over medium-high heat until very hot. Sprinkle salt and pepper on both sides of patties.

5 Place patties on hot grill rack. Cook 8 to 12 minutes for medium, or until desired doneness is reached, turning over once.

6 Meanwhile, puree red peppers and mayonnaise in blender until smooth. Place burgers on buns and top with cheese and red pepper sauce.

....

EACH SERVING: ABOUT 560 CALORIES, 35G PROTEIN, 27G CARBOHYDRATE, 33G TOTAL FAT (14G SATURATED), 3G FIBER, 120MG CHOLESTEROL, 1,097MG SODIUM.

TIP

Manchego, a slightly sweet and nutty-tasting sheep's milk cheese from the La Mancha region of Spain, can range in flavor depending on how long it has aged. Our pick is a young manchego, which has been aged for 6 months or less. Its supple and moist texture makes it a great melting cheese.

Pepper & Onion
CHEESEBURGERS

A quick sauté of sweet red onions and bell peppers
gives these burgers a blast of flavor and
extra moistness. Swap in Swiss or fontina cheese
for the Monterey Jack, if you wish.

ACTIVE TIME: 10 MINUTES   **TOTAL TIME:** 19 MINUTES
MAKES: 4 BURGERS

1¼ **pounds ground beef chuck**

½ **teaspoon coarsely ground black pepper**

¾ **teaspoon salt**

2 **tablespoons olive oil**

1 **red onion, sliced**

1 **red or yellow pepper, sliced**

4 **slices Monterey Jack cheese (about 3 ounces)**

4 **hamburger buns, split**

1 Divide ground beef into 4 mounds (about 5 ounces each), and loosely shape into balls.

2 Using your hands, gently flatten balls into ¾-inch-thick patties, handling meat as little as possible. Smooth patty edges with your fingers.

3 Place patties on a flat surface. Using your thumbs, press into centers of patties to make deep indentations. Refrigerate until ready to grill.

4 Prepare outdoor grill for covered direct grilling over medium-high heat, or heat ridged grill pan over medium-high heat until very hot. Sprinkle salt and pepper on both sides of patties.

5 Place patties on hot grill rack. Cook 8 to 12 minutes for medium, or until desired doneness is reached, turning over once. Top each burger with 1 slice cheese. Cover and cook until cheese has melted, about 1 minute longer.

6 Meanwhile, in 12-inch skillet, heat oil over medium-high heat until hot. Add red pepper and onion; cook, stirring occasionally, until vegetables are tender.

7 Place burgers on buns and top with pepper and onion mixture.

EACH SERVING: ABOUT 539 CALORIES, 35G PROTEIN, 26G CARBOHYDRATE, 32G TOTAL FAT (12G SATURATED), 2G FIBER, 105MG CHOLESTEROL, 857MG SODIUM.

Chicken Caesar
BURGERS

Hail Caesar! These yummy chicken and cheese burgers
are topped with grilled romaine lettuce and a
lemony anchovy-and-garlic sauce.

ACTIVE TIME: 20 MINUTES   **TOTAL TIME:** 32 MINUTES
MAKES: 4 BURGERS

CAESAR SAUCE

1   lemon

2   anchovy fillets, minced

1   small clove garlic, minced

⅓   cup light mayonnaise

¼   cup freshly grated Parmesan cheese

1   large heart romaine lettuce

1   tablespoon olive oil

¾   teaspoon salt

¼   cup freshly grated Parmesan cheese

½   teaspoon ground black pepper

1¼   pounds ground chicken or turkey

4   (4" by 4") squares focaccia bread
     (1-inch thick), each split horizontally in half
     and toasted

1   Prepare outdoor grill for direct grilling over
medium heat.

2   **For Caesar Sauce:** From lemon, grate
1 teaspoon peel and squeeze 2 tablespoons juice.
In small bowl, stir together lemon peel and juice,
anchovies, garlic, mayonnaise, and Parmesan
until blended. Set Caesar sauce aside. Makes
about ½ cup.

3   Cut romaine heart lengthwise into quarters.
Place romaine and any loose leaves on plate;
drizzle with oil and sprinkle with ¼ teaspoon
salt.

4   In medium bowl, combine ground chicken,
remaining ½ teaspoon salt, pepper, and
Parmesan until blended, but do not overmix.
Shape chicken mixture into 4 equal patties, each
about ¾-inch thick, handling mixture as little as
possible. Spray both sides of patties with nonstick
cooking spray.

5   Place patties on hot grill rack; cook 12 to 14
minutes or just until chicken loses its pink color
throughout, turning over once.

6   About 5 minutes before burgers are done, add
romaine to grill rack. Grill, turning occasionally,
until lightly browned and softened, about 5
minutes. Transfer romaine to platter as they are
done.

7   Serve burgers on focaccia and top with
romaine and Caesar sauce.

....

EACH SERVING: ABOUT 680 CALORIES, 42G PROTEIN,
54G CARBOHYDRATE, 33G TOTAL FAT (2G SATURATED),
4G FIBER, 25MG CHOLESTEROL, 1,550MG SODIUM.

Bacon-Wrapped
CHEESEBURGERS

How do you make a cheeseburger even better?
Wrap the patty in bacon, stick to Cheddar,
and slather the top with smoked paprika ketchup.

ACTIVE TIME: 15 MINUTES   TOTAL TIME: 28 MINUTES
MAKES: 4 BURGERS

⅓ cup ketchup

¼ teaspoon smoked paprika

8 slices bacon

1¼ pounds lean (85%) ground beef

¼ teaspoon salt

¼ teaspoon ground black pepper

4 slices Cheddar cheese (about 3 ounces)

4 hamburger buns, toasted

4 Boston lettuce leaves

1 Prepare outdoor grill for covered direct grilling over medium heat.

2 In small bowl, stir together ketchup and paprika until blended; set aside.

3 On plate, arrange 4 slices bacon in single layer between paper towels. Microwave on high 2 minutes or until some fat has rendered; transfer to cutting board and let cool. Repeat with remaining 4 slices bacon.

4 Shape ground beef into 4 equal patties, each ¾-inch thick, handling meat as little as possible. Sprinkle salt and pepper on both sides of patties. Crisscross each patty with 2 strips bacon. Place, seam side down, on large plate.

5 Place patties on hot grill rack. Cover and cook about 7 minutes for medium, or until desired doneness is reached, turning over once. Top each burger with 1 slice cheese. Cover and cook until cheese has melted, about 1 minute longer. Place burgers on buns and top with paprika ketchup and lettuce.

EACH SERVING: ABOUT 555 CALORIES, 40G PROTEIN, 27G CARBOHYDRATE, 31G TOTAL FAT (12G SATURATED), 1G FIBER, 124MG CHOLESTEROL, 1,150MG SODIUM.

TIP

These burgers are equally tasty with Muenster, mozzarella, or Monterey Jack cheese.

PATTY **Melts**

We make a classic stovetop burger even more delicious
by cooking the patties on the grill.

ACTIVE TIME: 10 MINUTES   **TOTAL TIME:** 18 MINUTES
MAKES: 4 BURGERS

1½ pounds ground beef chuck

½ teaspoon salt

½ teaspoon ground black pepper

1 large onion (10 to 12 ounces), cut crosswise
  into 5 thick slices

4 slices Swiss cheese (1 ounce each)

2 tablespoons Dijon mustard with seeds

4 slices rye bread

1 Prepare outdoor grill for covered direct grilling
over medium heat, or lightly spray a ridged grill
pan with nonstick cooking spray and place over
medium heat until hot.

2 Shape ground beef into 4 equal patties to
match bread, each ½-inch thick, handling meat
as little as possible. Sprinkle salt and pepper on
both sides of patties.

3 Place patties and onion slices on hot grill rack.
Cover and cook 8 to 10 minutes for medium, or
until desired doneness is reached, and until onion
is tender and browned, turning patties and onion
slices over once. About 2 minutes before burgers
are done, top each burger with 1 slice cheese.

4 To serve, spread mustard on 1 side of each
bread slice. Top each slice with a patty and some
grilled onion, separating onion slices into rings.

....

EACH SERVING: ABOUT 539 CALORIES, 41G PROTEIN,
25G CARBOHYDRATE, 30G TOTAL FAT (13G SATURATED),
3G FIBER, 128MG CHOLESTEROL, 773MG SODIUM.

CHEESY BURGERS

Buffalo Chicken
BURGERS

These zesty burgers with cool and creamy blue cheese sauce are sure to satisfy the most ardent Buffalo chicken fans.

ACTIVE TIME: 15 MINUTES **TOTAL TIME:** 27 MINUTES
MAKES: 4 BURGERS

¼ cup light mayonnaise

¼ cup reduced-fat sour cream

2 ounces blue cheese, crumbled (½ cup)

2 teaspoons cider vinegar

½ teaspoon Worcestershire sauce

1¼ pounds ground chicken or turkey

1 large stalk celery, finely chopped

3 tablespoons cayenne pepper sauce, plus additional for serving (optional)

4 hamburger buns, split and toasted

lettuce leaves

carrot and celery sticks

1 Prepare outdoor grill for direct grilling over medium heat.

2 In small bowl, stir together mayonnaise, sour cream, blue cheese, vinegar, and Worcestershire sauce until blended. Set blue cheese sauce aside. Makes about ¾ cup.

3 In medium bowl, combine ground chicken, celery, and cayenne pepper sauce until blended, but do not overmix. Shape chicken mixture into 4 equal patties, each about ¾-inch thick, handling mixture as little as possible. Spray both sides of patties with nonstick cooking spray.

4 Place patties on hot grill rack; cook 12 to 14 minutes or just until chicken loses its pink color throughout, turning over once.

5 Serve burgers on buns with lettuce and some blue cheese sauce. Serve remaining blue cheese sauce with carrot and celery sticks. Pass additional cayenne pepper sauce to serve with burgers, if using.

EACH SERVING: ABOUT 345 CALORIES, 27G PROTEIN, 22G CARBOHYDRATE, 16G TOTAL FAT (1G SATURATED), 1G FIBER, 0MG CHOLESTEROL, 785MG SODIUM.

EACH TABLESPOON BLUE CHEESE SAUCE: ABOUT 40 CALORIES, 1G PROTEIN, 1G CARBOHYDRATE, 4G TOTAL FAT (2G SATURATED), 0G FIBER, 7MG CHOLESTEROL, 110MG SODIUM.

TIP

Cayenne pepper sauce is a milder variety of hot pepper sauce that adds tang and flavor, not just heat. It can be found in the condiments section, near the ketchup, in the supermarket.

TURKEY CHEESEBURGERS
with Grilled Sweet Onion

Grilled onion makes an outstanding cheeseburger topping.
To make things easy, thread each slice through a skewer
so the onion won't fall through the grill rack while cooking.

ACTIVE TIME: 10 MINUTES **TOTAL TIME:** 22 MINUTES
MAKES: 4 BURGERS

1¼ **pounds ground turkey**

½ **teaspoon coarsely ground black pepper**

1 **teaspoon salt**

4 **slices sweet onion, such as Vidalia or Maui (each ½-inch thick)**

4 **slices Muenster cheese (about 3 ounces)**

4 **green-leaf lettuce leaves**

2 **medium tomatoes (6 to 8 ounces each), thinly sliced**

4 **hamburger buns, split and toasted**

1 Soak 4 (12-inch) bamboo skewers in *hot water to cover*, at least 30 minutes. Meanwhile, prepare outdoor grill for direct grilling over medium heat.
2 Shape ground turkey into 4 equal patties, each about ¾-inch thick, handling meat as little as possible. Sprinkle pepper and ¾ teaspoon salt on both sides of patties. Spray both sides of patties with nonstick cooking spray.

3 Thread 1 skewer through center of each onion slice. Sprinkle onion with remaining ¼ teaspoon salt.
4 Place onion and patties on hot grill rack; cook onion 8 to 10 minutes or until browned and tender, turning over once. Cook burgers 12 to 14 minutes or just until turkey loses its pink color throughout, turning over once. About 1 minute before burgers are done, top each burger with 1 slice cheese.
5 Serve burgers on buns and top with lettuce, tomato, and grilled onion.

. . . .

EACH SERVING: ABOUT 446 CALORIES, 37G PROTEIN, 31G CARBOHYDRATE, 19G TOTAL FAT (7G SATURATED), 3G FIBER, 115MG CHOLESTEROL, 1,017MG SODIUM.

 TIP

If you have metal skewers, you can skip the soaking in step 1.

CHEESY BURGERS

GREEK
Chicken Burgers

Yogurt, feta, and mint add a taste of the Aegean
to these flavorful mini burgers served in pita pockets.

ACTIVE TIME: 20 MINUTES   **TOTAL TIME:** 30 MINUTES
MAKES: 8 MINI BURGERS (4 MAIN-DISH SERVINGS)

4   pitas (6 inches each) with pockets

1   pound ground chicken

2   ounces crumbled feta cheese (½ cup)

1   large egg

2/3   cup loosely packed fresh mint leaves,
     chopped

¼   teaspoon salt

⅛   teaspoon ground black pepper

1   container (6 ounces) low-fat plain yogurt

4   cups thinly sliced romaine or iceberg lettuce

3   plum tomatoes, sliced

1 Cut off ⅓ piece from each pita and grate on fine side of grater or pulse in food processor to make ½ cup breadcrumbs.

2 In large bowl, combine crumbs, ground chicken, feta, egg, ¼ cup mint, salt, and pepper until blended, but do not overmix. Shape chicken mixture into 8 equal patties, each about ¾-inch thick, handling mixture as little as possible.

3 Lightly spray 12-inch nonstick skillet with nonstick cooking spray and heat over medium heat until hot. Add patties and cook 10 to 12 minutes or just until chicken loses its pink color throughout, turning over once.

4 Meanwhile, in small bowl, combine yogurt and remaining mint.

5 To serve, fill each pita with lettuce, tomatoes, 2 burgers, and yogurt sauce.

···

EACH SERVING: ABOUT 430 CALORIES, 33G PROTEIN, 38G CARBOHYDRATE, 16G TOTAL FAT (4G SATURATED), 4G FIBER, 73MG CHOLESTEROL, 750MG SODIUM.

Smothered Swiss
TURKEY BURGERS

To make these cheesy burgers even more indulgent,
we've topped them with a fabulous mushroom cream sauce.

ACTIVE TIME: 10 MINUTES   **TOTAL TIME:** 30 MINUTES

MAKES: 4 BURGERS

- 2   shallots, quartered
- 1   package (10 ounces) sliced mushrooms
- 1   pound ground turkey
- 3/4 teaspoon salt
- 1   tablespoon olive oil
- 4   slices Swiss cheese (about 3 ounces)
- 1   tablespoon butter or margarine
- 1   tablespoon all-purpose flour
- 1   cup beef broth
- 1   tablespoon heavy or whipping cream
- 1/4 teaspoon ground black pepper
- 4   hamburger buns, split and toasted

1 In food processor with knife blade attached, pulse shallots until chopped; remove half to small bowl. To processor, add ½ package mushrooms to remaining shallots; pulse into bits.

2 In large bowl, combine mushroom mixture, ground turkey, and ½ teaspoon salt until blended, but do not overmix. Shape turkey mixture into 4 equal patties, handling mixture as little as possible.

3 In 12-inch skillet, heat oil over medium-high heat until hot. Add patties and cook 8 to 10 minutes or just until turkey loses its pink color throughout, turning once. Transfer burgers to plate. Top each with 1 slice cheese; keep warm.

4 In same skillet, melt butter over medium heat. Add remaining shallot and remaining mushrooms; cook 5 minutes. Stir in flour; cook 30 seconds. Add broth; cook until thickened, about 5 minutes. Stir in cream, remaining ¼ teaspoon salt, and pepper. Place burgers on buns and top with sauce.

EACH SERVING: ABOUT 455 CALORIES, 33G PROTEIN, 27G CARBOHYDRATE, 24G TOTAL FAT (9G SATURATED), 2G FIBER, 115MG CHOLESTEROL, 910MG SODIUM.

TIP

For an even bolder-tasting sauce, use a package of sliced cremini mushrooms.

Spicy Shrimp Sliders
(page 101)

5 Deep Sea Burgers

If you're a fish lover, here's a golden opportunity to reel in a fabulous burger from the sea. For best results, stick to sturdy, meaty fish like salmon, tuna, and shrimp. Our catch includes Asian Tuna Burgers (page 104) with fresh ginger, soy sauce, and green onions; Fresh Salmon Burgers with Capers & Dill (page 93); plus Spicy Shrimp Sliders (page 101), zipped up with garlic and smoked paprika. We'll even show you how to make a brilliant burger out of canned fish.

Chopping fresh salmon and tuna by hand will yield the lightest, most tender burgers. If using a food processor, pulse just until coarsely chopped. Fish patties are delicate, so chill the patties at least 30 minutes to help them keep their shape while cooking (this particularly helps with grilled fish burgers). To ensure fish burgers stay nice and moist, avoid overcooking—when a burger is slightly pink inside, it's done.

FRESH SALMON BURGERS
with Capers & Dill

If you've never made grilled salmon burgers before,
try this simple recipe with a zingy lemon and caper sauce.

ACTIVE TIME: 25 MINUTES   **TOTAL TIME:** 31 MINUTES
MAKES: 4 BURGERS

1   large lemon

¼   cup light mayonnaise

1   tablespoon capers, drained and coarsely
    chopped

1   pound skinless salmon fillet

¼   cup loosely packed fresh dill, chopped

2   green onions, thinly sliced

½   cup plain dried breadcrumbs

¾   teaspoon salt

4   whole wheat hamburger buns, split and
    toasted

green-leaf lettuce leaves

1   Prepare outdoor grill for direct grilling over
medium heat.

2   Meanwhile, from lemon, grate 1 teaspoon peel
and squeeze 1 tablespoon juice.

3   In small bowl, stir together lemon juice and
½ teaspoon lemon peel with mayonnaise and
capers until blended. Set lemon-caper sauce
aside. Makes about ⅓ cup.

4   With large chef's knife, finely chop salmon;
place in medium bowl. Add dill, green onions,
¼ cup breadcrumbs, salt, and remaining
½ teaspoon lemon peel to salmon; gently mix
with fork until combined. Shape salmon mixture
into four 3-inch round patties.

5   Sprinkle both sides of patties with remaining
¼ cup breadcrumbs. Spray both sides of patties
with nonstick cooking spray.

6   Place patties on hot grill rack; cook 6 to 8
minutes, or until browned on the outside and still
slightly pink in the center for medium, or until
desired doneness is reached, turning over once.

7   Serve burgers on buns with lettuce and lemon-
caper mayonnaise.

EACH SERVING: ABOUT 380 CALORIES, 27G PROTEIN,
34G CARBOHYDRATE, 15G TOTAL FAT (3G SATURATED),
3G FIBER, 65MG CHOLESTEROL, 990MG SODIUM.

SALMON BURGERS
with Cucumber-Yogurt Sauce

Cottage cheese and eggs make these burgers extra
moist and tender. They can be served with or without the bun
and are topped with a garlicky-yogurt sauce.

ACTIVE TIME: 25 MINUTES   TOTAL TIME: 33 MINUTES
MAKES: 4 BURGERS

CUCUMBER-YOGURT SAUCE

- ½ cup fat-free plain yogurt
- 1 tablespoon fresh lemon juice
- 1 teaspoon finely chopped garlic
- ½ teaspoon salt
- ¼ teaspoon ground black pepper
- 1 tablespoon chopped fresh dill
- ¼ English cucumber, grated and squeezed dry (¼ cup)

BURGERS

- 1½ pounds skinless salmon fillet
- 1 medium shallot, finely chopped (¼ cup)
- 2 teaspoons chopped fresh dill
- 1 tablespoon fresh lemon juice
- 2 tablespoons fat-free cottage cheese
- 2 large egg yolks, lightly beaten
- ¾ teaspoon salt
- ¼ teaspoon ground black pepper
- 2 teaspoons olive oil

hamburger buns, lettuce, and sliced tomatoes (optional)

1 **Prepare Cucumber-Yogurt Sauce:** In small bowl, combine yogurt, lemon juice, garlic, salt, and pepper until blended. Stir in dill and cucumber. Cover and refrigerate until ready to serve.

2 **Prepare Burgers:** With large chef's knife, finely chop salmon; place in medium bowl. Add shallot, dill, lemon juice, cottage cheese, egg yolks, salt, and pepper; gently mix with fork until well blended. Shape salmon mixture into 4 equal patties, each ¾-inch thick.

3 In 12-inch nonstick skillet, heat oil over medium heat until hot. Add patties and cook 8 to 10 minutes or until browned on the outside and just opaque throughout, turning over once.

4 Place burgers on buns and top with lettuce and tomatoes, if using. Serve with yogurt sauce.

EACH SERVING: ABOUT 399 CALORIES, 42G PROTEIN, 27G CARBOHYDRATE, 12G TOTAL FAT (3G SATURATED), 1G FIBER, 173MG CHOLESTEROL, 1,079MG SODIUM.

TIP

Double the Cucumber Yogurt Sauce and stash the extras in the fridge. It makes a great dip for crudités.

SALMON BURGERS
with Cajun Rémoulade Sauce

Lemon and chopped parsley add delicate flavor
to these easy burgers. Serve with thinly sliced cucumbers
and a dollop of our zesty rémoulade sauce.

ACTIVE TIME: 20 MINUTES　　TOTAL TIME: 30 MINUTES
MAKES: 4 BURGERS

CAJUN RÉMOULADE SAUCE

- ⅓ cup light mayonnaise
- 2 tablespoons chili sauce
- 2 teaspoons spicy brown mustard
- 1 teaspoon Worcestershire sauce
- 2 green onions, minced
- ⅛ teaspoon cayenne (ground red) pepper

BURGERS

- 1 pound skinless salmon fillet
- ½ cup loosely packed fresh parsley leaves, chopped
- 2 teaspoons grated lemon peel
- ½ teaspoon salt
- ¼ teaspoon coarsely ground black pepper
- ¼ cup plain dried breadcrumbs
- 1 tablespoon olive oil
- 4 hamburger buns, warmed

1 **Prepare Cajun Rémoulade Sauce:** In small bowl, stir together mayonnaise, chili sauce, mustard, Worcestershire sauce, green onions, and cayenne pepper until blended. Makes about ½ cup.

2 **Prepare Burgers:** With large chef's knife, finely chop salmon; place in medium bowl. Add parsley, lemon peel, salt, and black pepper to salmon; gently mix with fork until combined. Shape salmon mixture into four 3-inch round patties.

3 Place breadcrumbs on waxed paper. Carefully dip patties, one at a time, into crumbs, turning to coat both sides.

4 In 10-inch nonstick skillet, heat oil over medium heat until hot. Add patties and cook 10 minutes or until browned on the outside and still slightly pink in the center for medium, or until desired doneness is reached, turning over once. Serve burgers on buns and top with Cajun Rémoulade Sauce.

....

EACH SERVING: ABOUT 393 CALORIES, 28G PROTEIN, 32G CARBOHYDRATE, 16G TOTAL FAT (3G SATURATED), 2G FIBER, 60MG CHOLESTEROL, 891MG SODIUM.

 TIP

You can cover and refrigerate the sauce up to 3 days ahead.

SALMON BURGERS
with Lemon-Basil Mayo

These scrumptious burgers, studded with fresh corn
from the cob, are topped with a lemony basil mayo
for the perfect summer sammie.

ACTIVE TIME: 20 MINUTES   TOTAL TIME: 26 MINUTES
MAKES: 4 BURGERS

2   ears corn, husks and silk removed

1   pound skinless salmon fillet

3   green onions, thinly sliced

1   large egg white

½   cup plain dried breadcrumbs

¾   teaspoon salt

1   teaspoon finely grated lemon peel

¼   cup mayonnaise

1   tablespoon chopped fresh basil

4   hamburger buns, split

Bibb lettuce leaves, for topping

1   Prepare outdoor grill for direct grilling over
medium heat.

2   Meanwhile, cut kernels from cobs of corn;
place in large bowl. With large chef's knife, finely
chop salmon; add to bowl. With fork, gently mix
in green onions, egg white, ¼ cup breadcrumbs,
salt, and ½ teaspoon lemon peel. Firmly pack
salmon mixture into four 3½-inch patties; dredge
in remaining ¼ cup breadcrumbs and spray both
sides with nonstick cooking spray.

3   Place patties on hot grill rack. Cook 6 to 8
minutes or until browned on the outside and still
slightly pink in the center for medium, or until
desired doneness is reached, turning over once.

4   Meanwhile, in small bowl, stir together
mayonnaise, basil, and remaining ½ teaspoon
lemon peel until blended.

5   Serve burgers on buns with lettuce and lemon-
basil mayonnaise.

EACH SERVING: ABOUT 515 CALORIES, 35G PROTEIN,
42G CARBOHYDRATE, 23G TOTAL FAT (4G SATURATED),
3G FIBER, 77MG CHOLESTEROL, 910MG SODIUM.

TIP

If desired, swap in fresh tarragon for the
basil.

Salmon-Horseradish
BURGERS

Looking for a pantry-friendly burger?
We've dressed up canned salmon with prepared horseradish
and a touch of soy sauce for a perfect weeknight meal.

ACTIVE TIME: 10 MINUTES   TOTAL TIME: 20 MINUTES
MAKES: 4 BURGERS

1   can (14½ ounces) red or pink salmon, drained
    and flaked

1   green onion, sliced

3   tablespoons prepared white horseradish

2   tablespoons plain dried breadcrumbs

1   teaspoon soy sauce

¼   teaspoon coarsely ground black pepper

4   hamburger buns, split

lettuce leaves, for topping

1 In medium bowl, lightly mix salmon, green onion, horseradish, breadcrumbs, soy sauce, and pepper with fork. Shape salmon mixture into four 3-inch round patties. Spray both sides of patties with nonstick cooking spray.

2 Spray 12-inch nonstick skillet with nonstick cooking spray and heat over medium heat until hot. Add salmon patties and cook about 10 minutes or until golden and hot, turning over once. Serve on buns and top with lettuce.

EACH SERVING: ABOUT 255 CALORIES, 19G PROTEIN, 26G CARBOHYDRATE, 9G TOTAL FAT (2G SATURATED), 2G FIBER, 50MG CHOLESTEROL, 815MG SODIUM.

TIP

Canned red salmon is prized for its rich taste, deep red color, and firm texture. Less pricey pink salmon is more delicately flavored.

Teriyaki Salmon
BURGERS

When you start with fresh salmon, it doesn't take
a laundry list of ingredients to make a fabulous burger.
Take this recipe for example—it utilizes just
teriyaki sauce, green onions, and fresh ginger.

ACTIVE TIME: 15 MINUTES   TOTAL TIME: 25 MINUTES
MAKES: 4 BURGERS

5   sesame-seed hamburger buns
1   pound skinless salmon fillet
2   tablespoons teriyaki sauce
2   medium green onions, chopped
1½ teaspoons grated, peeled fresh ginger

1   Coarsely grate 1 hamburger bun to make
breadcrumbs. Measure out ⅓ cup breadcrumbs
and set aside. Reserve remaining crumbs to coat
patties.

2   With large chef's knife, finely chop salmon;
place in medium bowl. Add teriyaki sauce,
green onions, ginger, and ⅓ cup breadcrumbs to
salmon; gently mix with fork until combined.

3   On waxed paper, shape salmon mixture into
four 3-inch round patties. Coat both sides of
patties with reserved breadcrumbs.

4   Split remaining 4 hamburger buns. Spray
10-inch nonstick skillet with nonstick cooking
spray and heat over medium heat until hot. Add
patties and cook 10 minutes or until browned on
the outside and still slightly pink in the center for
medium, or until desired doneness is reached,
turning over once. Serve burgers on buns.

. . . .

EACH SERVING: ABOUT 340 CALORIES, 28G PROTEIN,
38G CARBOHYDRATE, 12G TOTAL FAT (2G SATURATED),
2G FIBER, 61MG CHOLESTEROL, 695MG SODIUM.

TIP

If you want to skip fresh salmon, substitute
a 14½-ounce can of red or pink salmon,
drained and flaked, and add 1 large egg to
the mixture.

SALMON **Sliders**

Red wine is the surprise ingredient in
these sophisticated sliders. Serve them with
a side of creamy potato salad or coleslaw.

ACTIVE TIME: 15 MINUTES   TOTAL TIME: 30 MINUTES

MAKES: 12 SLIDERS

¾ cup dry red wine

6 hot dog buns

1 pound skinless salmon fillet, cut into chunks

2 green onions, chopped

2 tablespoons plus ⅓ cup mayonnaise

¼ teaspoon salt

¼ teaspoon ground black pepper

1 Preheat oven to 425°F. Line baking pan with foil.

2 Meanwhile, in small saucepan, boil ½ cup wine over high heat until reduced by half, stirring; chill slightly. Toast 2 hot dog buns and cool.

3 In food processor with knife blade attached, pulse toasted buns into crumbs; transfer to large bowl. To processor, add salmon and pulse until chopped; place in bowl with crumbs. Add green onions, remaining ¼ cup wine, 2 tablespoons mayonnaise, salt, and pepper; gently mix with fork until combined. Shape salmon mixture into 12 equal patties.

4 Place patties on prepared pan and bake 10 minutes or until cooked through.

5 Toast remaining 4 buns; cut into thirds. Whisk chilled wine into remaining ⅓ cup mayonnaise until blended. Place burgers on buns and top with red wine mayonnaise.

EACH SLIDER: ABOUT 168 CALORIES, 10G PROTEIN, 11G CARBOHYDRATE, 9G TOTAL FAT (1G SATURATED), 1G FIBER, 21MG CHOLESTEROL, 228MG SODIUM.

Spicy Shrimp SLIDERS

These mini burgers are made to party!
Seasoned with Italian herbs and smoked paprika,
these sautéed patties are topped with a quickie carrot slaw
and basil mayonnaise. For photo, see page 90.

For photo, see page 90.

ACTIVE TIME: 25 MINUTES   **TOTAL TIME:** 33 MINUTES
MAKES: 12 SLIDERS

1   lemon

2   medium carrots, shredded

¼   cup fresh basil leaves, chopped

¼   cup mayonnaise

1   tablespoon Dijon mustard

salt

1¼ pounds shrimp, peeled and deveined

3   cloves garlic, crushed with garlic press

1   teaspoon smoked paprika

¾   cup dried Italian breadcrumbs

¼   teaspoon ground black pepper

4   tablespoons vegetable oil

12   slider buns, split

1   Grate peel from lemon into large bowl.

2   Squeeze 2 tablespoons lemon juice into medium bowl; stir in carrots, basil, mayonnaise, mustard, and pinch of salt.

3   In food processor with knife blade attached, pulse shrimp until chopped, stirring occasionally. Transfer three-fourths of shrimp to bowl with peel; process remaining shrimp until mostly smooth and add to same bowl. Add garlic, paprika, ¼ cup breadcrumbs, ¼ teaspoon salt, and pepper; gently mix with hands until blended.

4   Shape shrimp mixture into 12 equal patties, each about ½-inch thick. Coat both sides of patties with remaining ½ cup breadcrumbs.

5   In 12-inch skillet, heat 2 tablespoons oil over medium-high heat until hot. Add 6 patties; cook 2 minutes per side or until cooked through, adjusting heat as necessary. Transfer to plate and keep warm. Repeat with remaining 2 tablespoons oil and 6 patties. Place burgers on buns and top with carrot slaw and basil mayonnaise.

....

EACH SLIDER: ABOUT 215 CALORIES, 14G PROTEIN, 22G CARBOHYDRATE, 8G TOTAL FAT (1G SATURATED), 0G FIBER, 61MG CHOLESTEROL, 365MG SODIUM.

TIP

If you want to save some coin by shelling and deveining the shrimp yourself, buy 1½ pounds large shrimp.

DEEP SEA BURGERS

Dill Tuna
BURGERS

Canned tuna gets a tasty twist in these dill burgers
with jarred tartar sauce and (surprise!) crunchy potato chips.

ACTIVE TIME: 15 MINUTES   **TOTAL TIME:** 21 MINUTES
MAKES: 4 BURGERS

2   cans (5 ounces each) solid white tuna in water, drained

4   green onions, chopped

3   stalks celery, chopped

¾   cup whole wheat breadcrumbs

½   cup tartar sauce

¼   cup chopped fresh dill

1   tablespoon fresh lemon juice

1   teaspoon hot pepper sauce

½   teaspoon salt

¼   teaspoon ground black pepper

1   tablespoon extra-virgin olive oil

4   Bibb lettuce leaves

2   ounces reduced-fat potato chips (about 36 chips)

4   whole-grain hamburger buns, split and toasted

1   In large bowl, combine tuna, green onions, celery, breadcrumbs, ¼ cup tartar sauce, dill, lemon juice, pepper sauce, salt, and pepper until blended. Shape tuna mixture into 4 equal patties.

2   In 12-inch nonstick skillet, heat oil over medium-high heat until hot. Add patties and cook about 6 minutes or until heated through, turning over once.

3   Serve burgers on buns with lettuce, remaining ¼ cup tartar sauce, and potato chips.

....

EACH SERVING: ABOUT 408 CALORIES, 21G PROTEIN, 48G CARBOHYDRATE, 16G TOTAL FAT (3G SATURATED), 6G FIBER, 26MG CHOLESTEROL, 1,050MG SODIUM.

Asian Tuna
BURGERS

Simply seasoned with soy sauce and fresh ginger,
then grilled until the sesame-seed coating is crisp and golden,
this patty has what it takes to be your go-to tuna burger.

ACTIVE TIME: 20 MINUTES   TOTAL TIME: 25 MINUTES
MAKES: 4 BURGERS

1   tuna steak (about 1 pound)

1   green onion, thinly sliced

2   tablespoons reduced-sodium soy sauce

1   teaspoon grated, peeled fresh ginger

¼   teaspoon coarsely ground black pepper

¼   cup plain dried breadcrumbs

2   tablespoons sesame seeds

pickled ginger (optional)

1 Prepare outdoor grill for direct grilling over medium heat.

2 Meanwhile, with large chef's knife, finely chop tuna; place in medium bowl. Add green onion, soy sauce, ginger, and pepper; gently mix with fork until combined. Shape tuna mixture into four 3-inch round patties (mixture will be very soft and moist).

3 On waxed paper, combine breadcrumbs and sesame seeds. With hands, carefully press patties, one at a time, into breadcrumb mixture, turning to coat both sides. Spray both sides of patties with nonstick cooking spray.

4 Place patties on hot grill rack. Cover and cook 5 to 6 minutes or until browned on the outside and still slightly pink in the center for medium-rare, turning over once. (If you prefer well-done, cook 2 to 3 minutes longer.) Serve with pickled ginger, if using.

EACH SERVING: ABOUT 210 CALORIES, 26G PROTEIN, 7G CARBOHYDRATE, 8G TOTAL FAT (2G SATURATED), 1G FIBER, 38MG CHOLESTEROL, 400MG SODIUM.

TUNA BURGERS
with Tomato-Basil Salsa

Canned tuna is mixed with white beans and fresh basil
to make these delicious patties.

ACTIVE TIME: 20 MINUTES   TOTAL TIME: 28 MINUTES
MAKES: 4 BURGERS

5   slices crusty Italian bread (each 1-inch thick)

1   can (6 ounces) tuna in olive oil

1   can (15 to 19 ounces) white kidney beans
    (cannellini), rinsed and drained

1   large bunch fresh basil leaves, chopped
    (about 1½ cups)

¾   teaspoon salt

coarsely ground black pepper

2   medium tomatoes, finely chopped

1   Into medium bowl, tear 1 slice bread into
¼-inch pieces. Reserve remaining bread to toast
later.

2   Drain tuna, reserving 1 teaspoon olive oil.
Place tuna in bowl with bread; add beans, 1 cup
basil, ½ teaspoon salt, and ¼ teaspoon pepper.
With potato masher or fork, mix until evenly
blended and most of beans are mashed. With
hands, shape mixture into four 3-inch round
patties.

3   In 12-inch nonstick skillet, heat reserved olive
oil over medium heat until hot. Add patties and
cook 8 to 10 minutes or until golden and heated
through, turning over once.

4   Meanwhile, in small bowl, toss tomatoes with
remaining ½ cup basil, remaining ¼ teaspoon
salt, and ⅛ teaspoon pepper; set aside tomato
salsa.

5   Toast reserved bread slices. Serve each burger
on a toasted bread slice and topped with tomato-
basil salsa.

EACH SERVING: ABOUT 335 CALORIES, 21G PROTEIN,
50G CARBOHYDRATE, 5G TOTAL FAT (1G SATURATED),
8G FIBER, 6MG CHOLESTEROL, 1,000MG SODIUM.

DEEP SEA BURGERS

Portobello Pesto Burgers
(page 113)

6 Veggie Burgers

News flash! Those nondescript meatless stand-ins for a hamburger are a thing of the past. Our thoroughly modern veggie burgers are so easy and delicious, they challenge beef's place on the bun. We've got meatless masterpieces with grains to choose from, like our DIY Veggie Burgers (page 109). Or if beans are your thing, there are pinto, black, and garbanzo bean burgers. We even share how to cook beans from scratch—and why it's worth it.

If you're looking for the ultimate mushroom burger, our Portobello Pesto Burgers (page 113) are so thick and juicy, the gang may mistake them for steak. And if you're thinking beyond Meatless Monday, our Vegetarian Rice & Bean Burgers (page 119) and zesty Black Bean Burgers (page 116) freeze beautifully, so you can enjoy a bonus burger dinner any day of the week.

DIY **Veggie Burgers**

These multigrain mushroom-walnut burgers are so tasty, even non-vegetarians will love them. Make the whole recipe for a crowd, or freeze half the burgers for another speedy meal.

ACTIVE TIME: 40 MINUTES   **TOTAL TIME:** 1 HOUR
MAKES: 8 BURGERS

- ½ cup bulgur
- ¾ cup old-fashioned oats, uncooked
- 1 tablespoon olive oil
- 1 medium onion (6 to 8 ounces), finely chopped
- 1 package (10 ounces) mushrooms, finely chopped
- ½ cup walnuts, finely chopped
- 2 cloves garlic, crushed with garlic press
- 1 carrot, cut up
- 1 stalk celery, cut up
- ¼ cup packed fresh parsley leaves
- ⅛ teaspoon dried thyme
- 1 large egg white
- 3 ounces Cheddar cheese, shredded (½ cup)
- ½ teaspoon salt
- ½ teaspoon ground black pepper
- hamburger buns, lettuce, tomato, and red onion (optional)

1 In microwave-safe medium bowl, microwave *1 cup water* and bulgur on high, 5 to 7 minutes or until liquid is absorbed.

2 In 12-inch nonstick skillet, toast oats over medium heat, 3 minutes. Transfer to food processor.

3 In same skillet, heat oil over medium heat until hot. Add onion; cook, stirring, 7 minutes. Add mushrooms, walnuts, and garlic; cook, stirring, until liquid evaporates, about 8 minutes.

4 In food processor with knife blade attached, pulse oats, carrot, celery, parsley, and thyme until finely chopped. Add egg white, Cheddar, bulgur, mushroom mixture, salt, and pepper. Pulse until well combined.

5 Scoop ½ cup mixture and pat into a 3½-inch round. Place on waxed paper; repeat. (Wrap and refrigerate up to 3 days or freeze up to 3 months. Do not thaw before cooking.)

6 Wipe same skillet clean; spray with nonstick cooking spray, then heat over medium heat, 1 minute. Add burgers in 2 batches; cook 10 to 12 minutes or until browned, turning once. Serve burgers on buns with lettuce, tomato, and onion, if using.

....

EACH SERVING: ABOUT 195 CALORIES, 8G PROTEIN, 18G CARBOHYDRATE, 11G TOTAL FAT (3G SATURATED), 4G FIBER, 11MG CHOLESTEROL, 230MG SODIUM.

Pinto Bean
BURGERS

Canned chipotle chiles (smoked jalapeños packed in a thick vinegary sauce called adobo), plus a slice of pickled jalapeño give these tasty burgers a double dose of heat.

ACTIVE TIME: 15 MINUTES   TOTAL TIME: 23 MINUTES
MAKES: 4 BURGERS

1   can (15 to 15½ ounces) pinto beans, rinsed and drained

1   teaspoon ground cumin

1   teaspoon canned chipotle chile in adobo, minced

1   slice pickled jalapeño chile, minced

2   tablespoons plus ½ cup mild salsa

5   tablespoons plain dried breadcrumbs

2   tablespoons olive oil

4   hamburger buns, warmed

4   lettuce leaves

fresh cilantro leaves, sliced red onion, and sour cream (optional)

1   In medium bowl, with potato masher, mash beans until almost smooth. Stir in cumin, chipotle, jalapeño, 2 tablespoons salsa, and 2 tablespoons breadcrumbs until combined.

2   Place remaining 3 tablespoons breadcrumbs on sheet of waxed paper. With floured hands, shape bean mixture into four 3-inch round burgers; coat with breadcrumbs.

3   In 12-inch nonstick skillet, heat oil over medium heat until hot. Add patties and cook about 8 minutes or until lightly browned and heated through, turning over once.

4   Place lettuce on bottom halves of buns; top with burgers, remaining ½ cup salsa, and tops of buns. Serve burgers with cilantro, red onion, and sour cream, if using.

EACH SERVING: ABOUT 350 CALORIES, 11G PROTEIN, 51G CARBOHYDRATE, 11G TOTAL FAT (2G SATURATED), 8G FIBER, 0MG CHOLESTEROL, 775MG SODIUM.

GRILLED VEGGIE BURGERS
with Avocado Salsa

We dress up frozen veggie burgers
with a super-quick avocado salsa and make it deluxe
by stuffing each sandwich with lettuce, tomato,
and alfalfa sprouts.

ACTIVE TIME: 10 MINUTES   TOTAL TIME: 15 MINUTES
MAKES: 4 BURGERS

- 1   ripe avocado
- 1   green onion, chopped
- 2   tablespoons medium salsa
- 1   teaspoon fresh lemon juice
- 1   tablespoon chopped fresh cilantro
- ¼   teaspoon salt
- 1   package (9½ ounces) frozen vegetarian soy burgers (4 burgers)
- 4   whole wheat hamburger buns, split and toasted
- 1   large tomato, sliced
- 4   green-leaf lettuce leaves
- 1   cup alfalfa sprouts

1 Prepare outdoor grill for covered direct grilling over medium-high heat.

2 In medium bowl, mash avocado; stir in green onion, salsa, lemon juice, cilantro, and salt.

3 Lightly spray both sides of burgers with nonstick cooking spray. Place burgers on hot grill rack; cover and cook, 3 minutes. Turn burgers over; cover and cook 2½ minutes longer. Burgers should reach an internal temperature of 160°F.

4 Serve burgers on buns with tomato, avocado salsa, and sprouts.

EACH SERVING: ABOUT 299 CALORIES, 19G PROTEIN, 34G CARBOHYDRATE, 13G TOTAL FAT (2G SATURATED), 12G FIBER, 5MG CHOLESTEROL, 825MG SODIUM.

TIP

For an even speedier recipe, prepare the burgers in a skillet as the label directs.

Portobello Pesto
BURGERS

If you're craving a thick and juicy veggie burger, nothing beats portobello mushrooms. Ours are roasted with sun-dried tomato pesto, then topped with goat cheese, basil, and a refreshing Carrot-Fennel Slaw. For photo, see page 106.

ACTIVE TIME: 20 MINUTES   **TOTAL TIME:** 45 MINUTES
MAKES: 4 BURGERS

PORTOBELLO BURGERS

- 4 portobello mushrooms (1 pound), stems trimmed
- ¼ cup sun-dried tomato pesto
- 4 whole-grain hamburger buns, split
- 1 large ripe tomato, cut into 8 slices
- 1 log (4 ounces) fresh goat cheese, cut crosswise into 8 slices
- 8 large fresh basil leaves

CARROT-FENNEL SLAW

- 2 cups shredded carrots
- 1 small fennel bulb (6 ounces), trimmed and thinly sliced
- ½ cup loosely packed fresh basil leaves, thinly sliced
- 2 teaspoons olive oil
- 1½ teaspoons cider vinegar
- ¼ teaspoon salt
- ⅛ teaspoon ground black pepper

1 **Prepare Portobello Burgers:** Preheat toaster oven to 425°F. Place portobellos on foil-lined toaster oven tray, rounded side up. Bake 14 minutes. Flip mushrooms; spread 1 tablespoon pesto evenly on each. Bake until mushrooms are just tender, about 10 minutes longer.

2 **Prepare Carrot-Fennel Slaw:** Meanwhile, in large bowl, mix carrots, fennel, basil, oil, vinegar, salt, and pepper until well combined.

3 Toast buns. Place 2 tomato slices on bottom of each bun. Top each with 1 portobello, 2 slices goat cheese, 2 basil leaves, and top of bun. Serve burgers with Carrot-Fennel Slaw.

....

EACH SERVING: ABOUT 345 CALORIES, 15G PROTEIN, 38G CARBOHYDRATE, 16G TOTAL FAT (6G SATURATED), 8G FIBER, 13MG CHOLESTEROL, 635MG SODIUM.

PLT BURGERS

This fire-seared portobello burger, slathered with basil mayo
on a ciabatta bun, is brawny enough for beef lovers.
Before grilling, brush the mushrooms with rosemary-garlic oil
for a rich, robust taste.

ACTIVE TIME: 20 MINUTES   **TOTAL TIME:** 29 MINUTES
MAKES: 4 BURGERS

1   teaspoon fresh rosemary leaves, finely
     chopped

1   garlic clove, crushed with garlic press

3   tablespoons olive oil

3   tablespoons light mayonnaise

2   tablespoons packed, finely chopped fresh
     basil leaves

4   large portobello mushroom caps

¼   teaspoon salt

¼   teaspoon ground black pepper

4   ciabatta or other crusty rolls, split

4   iceberg lettuce leaves

½   cup arugula (optional)

1   ounce shaved Parmesan cheese

4   large tomato slices

1   Prepare outdoor grill for direct grilling over
medium-high heat.

2   In small bowl, combine rosemary, garlic, and
oil. In another small bowl, combine mayonnaise
and basil.

3   Brush oil mixture all over mushrooms, and
then sprinkle them with salt and pepper.

4   Place ciabatta halves, cut sides down, and
mushrooms on hot grill rack. Cook ciabatta 3
minutes or until toasted, turning over once. Cook
mushrooms 6 to 8 minutes or until browned and
tender, turning over once. Transfer to cutting
board. Cut mushrooms at an angle into ½-inch
slices, keeping mushroom shape intact.

5   Spread basil mayonnaise on cut sides of
ciabatta. Divide lettuce and arugula (if using)
among bottom halves. Place 1 mushroom on top,
slightly fanning slices apart. Top with Parmesan,
tomato, and ciabatta tops.

EACH SERVING: ABOUT 436 CALORIES, 17G PROTEIN,
55G CARBOHYDRATE, 18G TOTAL FAT (3G SATURATED),
4G FIBER, 10MG CHOLESTEROL, 880MG SODIUM.

Black Bean
BURGERS

These spicy burgers with cumin and coriander
get their kick thanks to a slathering of chipotle mayo.

ACTIVE TIME: 15 MINUTES   **TOTAL TIME:** 20 MINUTES
MAKES: 4 BURGERS

¼ cup plain dried breadcrumbs

¼ teaspoon ground cumin

¼ teaspoon ground coriander

3 cups cooked black beans (see Use Your
 Beans, page 118) or 2 cans (15 ounces each)
 low-sodium black beans, rinsed and drained

4 tablespoons light mayonnaise

¼ teaspoon salt

¼ teaspoon ground black pepper

2 large stalks celery, finely chopped

1 chipotle chile in adobo, finely chopped

4 green-leaf lettuce leaves

4 whole wheat hamburger buns, toasted

4 slices tomato

1 In food processor with knife blade attached,
pulse breadcrumbs, cumin, coriander, two-thirds
of beans, 2 tablespoons mayonnaise, salt, and
pepper until well blended. Transfer to large
bowl. Stir in celery and remaining whole beans
until well combined. Shape mixture into 4 equal
patties.

2 Lightly spray 12-inch nonstick skillet with
nonstick cooking spray and heat over medium
heat, 1 minute. Add patties and cook 10 to 12
minutes or until browned, carefully turning once.

3 Meanwhile, in small bowl, combine chipotle
chile and remaining 2 tablespoons mayonnaise
until well mixed. Serve burgers on buns with
lettuce, tomatoes, and chipotle mayonnaise.

EACH SERVING: ABOUT 370 CALORIES, 18G PROTEIN,
59G CARBOHYDRATE, 8G TOTAL FAT (1G SATURATED),
14G FIBER, 5MG CHOLESTEROL, 725MG SODIUM.

TIP

For a bonus weeknight meal, make a
double batch and freeze the uncooked
burgers. Defrost 10 minutes, and then cook
until heated through, about 12 minutes,
turning once.

Use Your Beans

Serious about your veggie burger? For a bean burger, consider cooking them from scratch instead of popping open a can. Not only do scratch-cooked beans have an earthier flavor, they're creamier too. Translation: you'll make the best bean burger ever.

Here's how to cook a 1-pound bag of dried beans to perfection. (Note: A 15-ounce can of beans equals 1½ cups scratch-cooked beans.)

BUY

Head to a store with a high product turnover—older beans take longer to cook and are less flavorful and tougher in texture.

PREP

Sort through beans to remove small stones and debris. Place beans in colander and rinse well with cold water. Transfer to a large bowl and add enough cold water to cover by 2 inches. Cover and soak 12 to 24 hours at room temperature.

COOK

Drain beans in a colander and rinse well with cold water. Transfer to large pot and add enough cold water to cover beans by an inch. Heat to boiling. Skim off foam and reduce heat. Cover and simmer 30 minutes. Add ½ teaspoon salt. Continue simmering until beans are tender (about 45 to 75 minutes longer depending on the variety). Remove from heat and stir in ½ teaspoon salt. Cool.

STORE

Cover cooked beans with some of their cooking liquid and place in an airtight container (use a microwave-safe container and allow headspace if freezing). Keep in the refrigerator up to 5 days, or freeze up to 6 months. To thaw, microwave on high for 4 minutes, stirring halfway through. Drain, rinse, and proceed with your bean burger.

VEGETARIAN
Rice & Bean Burgers

Tahini (sesame-seed paste), garlic, and fennel seeds add subtle flavor to these satisfying burgers.

ACTIVE TIME: 20 MINUTES   **TOTAL TIME:** 30 MINUTES
MAKES: 8 MINI BURGERS (4 MAIN-DISH SERVINGS)

1   lemon

1   container (6 ounces) plain low-fat yogurt

4   tablespoons well-stirred tahini (sesame-seed paste)

3/4 teaspoon salt

1   package (8.8 ounces) pre-cooked whole-grain brown rice

1   can (15 to 19 ounces) garbanzo beans (chickpeas)

1   clove garlic, crushed with garlic press

1/2 teaspoon fennel seeds

4   burrito-size spinach or sun-dried tomato tortillas

2   medium carrots, shredded

2   plum tomatoes, thinly sliced

1   Kirby (pickling) cucumber, thinly sliced

1   Prepare outdoor grill for direct grilling over medium heat.

2   From lemon, grate 1½ teaspoons peel and squeeze 2 tablespoons juice. In small bowl, stir together lemon juice, yogurt, 2 tablespoons tahini, and ½ teaspoon salt until blended. Set yogurt sauce aside. Makes about ¾ cup.

3   Microwave rice as label directs; set aside.

4   Reserve ¼ cup liquid from beans. Rinse beans and drain well. In medium bowl, combine beans, lemon peel, garlic, fennel seeds, remaining ¼ teaspoon salt, remaining 2 tablespoons tahini, and reserved bean liquid. With potato masher, coarsely mash bean mixture until well blended but still lumpy. Add rice and continue to mash just until blended.

5   Shape bean mixture into 8 equal patties, each about 1-inch thick. Spray both sides of patties with nonstick cooking spray.

6   Place patties on hot grill rack. Cook 10 to 12 minutes or until burgers are well browned and heated through, turning over once.

7   To serve, place 2 burgers in center of each tortilla; top evenly with yogurt sauce and vegetables. Fold opposite sides of each tortilla over filling, and then fold ends over to form a package.

....

EACH SERVING: ABOUT 490 CALORIES, 15G PROTEIN, 83G CARBOHYDRATE, 11G TOTAL FAT (2G SATURATED), 10G FIBER, 3MG CHOLESTEROL, 1,260MG SODIUM.

TIP
Use 2 cups leftover cooked brown rice from Chinese take-out!

Bulgur Bean
BURGERS

Bulgur adds a wonderfully nutty flavor
to these Middle Eastern-style burgers seasoned with
allspice, cinnamon, cumin, and chopped fresh mint.

ACTIVE TIME: 25 MINUTES   TOTAL TIME: 32 MINUTES
MAKES: 4 BURGERS

- ¾ teaspoon salt
- ½ cup bulgur
- 1 can (15 to 19 ounces) reduced-sodium black beans, rinsed and drained
- 1 container (6 ounces) plain low-fat yogurt
- ¼ teaspoon ground allspice
- ¼ teaspoon ground cinnamon
- ¼ teaspoon ground cumin
- ¼ cup packed fresh mint leaves, chopped
- 1 small Kirby (pickling) cucumber, shredded (about ½ cup)
- ⅛ teaspoon ground black pepper
- 4 whole wheat hamburger buns, split
- 4 lettuce leaves
- 1 medium tomato, sliced

1 In 1-quart saucepan, heat *1 cup water* and ½ teaspoon salt to boiling over high heat. Stir in bulgur. Reduce heat to low; cover and simmer 10 to 12 minutes or until water is absorbed.

2 Meanwhile, in large bowl, with potato masher or fork, mash beans with 2 tablespoons yogurt until almost smooth. Stir in bulgur, allspice, cinnamon, cumin, and half of mint until combined. With lightly floured hands, shape bean mixture into four 3-inch round patties. Lightly spray both sides of patties with nonstick cooking spray.

3 Spray 12-inch nonstick skillet with cooking spray and heat over medium heat until hot. Add patties and cook 8 minutes or until lightly browned and heated through, turning over once.

4 Meanwhile, in small bowl, combine cucumber, remaining yogurt, remaining mint, remaining ¼ teaspoon salt, and pepper until blended. Makes about 1¼ cups.

5 Serve burgers on buns with lettuce and tomato; top with some yogurt sauce. Serve with remaining yogurt sauce.

EACH SERVING: ABOUT 295 CALORIES, 16G PROTEIN, 58G CARBOHYDRATE, 3G TOTAL FAT (1G SATURATED), 13G FIBER, 3MG CHOLESTEROL, 960MG SODIUM.

TIP

If Kirby cukes aren't available, swap in an English cucumber instead.

SOUTHWESTERN
Black Bean Burgers

These speedy bite-size burgers get their kick
from a splash of hot pepper sauce.

ACTIVE TIME: 10 MINUTES   TOTAL TIME: 16 MINUTES
MAKES: 4 BURGERS

1   can (15 to 19 ounces) black beans,
    rinsed and drained

6   tablespoons light mayonnaise

¼   cup packed fresh cilantro leaves, chopped

1   tablespoon plain dried breadcrumbs

½   teaspoon ground cumin

½   teaspoon hot pepper sauce

4   sesame hamburger buns, split and toasted

1   cup thinly sliced romaine lettuce

4   slices beefsteak tomato

thinly sliced cucumber (optional)

1   In large bowl, with potato masher or fork, mash beans with 2 tablespoons mayonnaise until almost smooth (some lumps of beans should remain). Stir in cilantro, breadcrumbs, cumin, and pepper sauce until combined.

2   With lightly floured hands, shape bean mixture into four equal patties. Spray both sides of patties with nonstick cooking spray.

3   Heat 12-inch skillet over medium heat until hot. Add patties and cook about 6 minutes or until heated through, turning over once.

4   Serve burgers on buns with remaining 4 tablespoons mayonnaise, lettuce, tomato, and cucumber, if using.

EACH SERVING: ABOUT 396 CALORIES, 15G PROTEIN, 50G CARBOHYDRATE, 12G TOTAL FAT (2G SATURATED), 10G FIBER, 8MG CHOLESTEROL, 770MG SODIUM.

Index

Note: Page numbers in *italics* indicate photos of recipes located separately from respective recipes.

Photography Credits

FRONT COVER: Getty Images: © Rita Maas
BACK COVER: Offset Images: © Con Poulos

© Monica Buck: 121

Deposit Photo: © Bhofack2 72; © Draghicich 83; © Brooke Fuller 44 (cheese); © Lucie Lang 34; © Margo555 51; © Marisha5 103; © Marilyna 116; © Monkeybusiness 93; © Mny-Jhee 60; © Pes1982 56; © Photomaru 50; © Spline_x 29; © Szakaly 118 (top); © Tombaky 105; © Ivonne Wierink 118 (bottom)

Getty Images: © Apaltynowicz 122, © Olena Gorbenko Delicious Food 65; © Maria Kallin 9; © Rita Maas 2; © Lauri Patterson 55; © James A. Sugar 21; © Tetra Images 17;

iStockphoto: © 4kodiak 23 (left); © Benimage 63; © Bonnie Caton 88; © Creativeye99 59; © Lachlan Currie 53; © Floortje 114; © Mark Gillow 26; © Hanis 38; © Red Helga 44 (apricot); © Hudiemm 99; © Lujing 96; © Tarp Magnus 87; © Mark542244 (avocado); © Mashuk 47; © Ragnarocks 66; © Roberto A Sanchez 23 (right); © Tsuji 112

© Francis Janisch: 24, 28, 32, 39, 46, 80, 92

© Kate Mathis: 18, 19, 20, 40, 43, 58, 70, 75, 76, 77, 78, 79, 97, 108, 117

© Con Poulos: 90

© Kate Sears: 6, 52, 68, 89, 106

Shutterstock: 44 (pepper); © Wavebreakmedia 10; © Smit 100

StockFood: © Condé Nast Collection 110; © Tina Rupp 36; © Amy Kalyn Sims 48

Studio D: Chris Ekert 7; Philip Friedman 86; Mike Garten 12, 15, 30, 62; Lara Robby 102

© Anna Williams: 115

Metric Conversion Charts

The recipes that appear in this cookbook use the standard United States method for measuring liquid and dry or solid ingredients (teaspoons, tablespoons, and cups). The information on this chart is provided to help cooks outside the U.S. successfully use these recipes. All equivalents are approximate.

METRIC EQUIVALENTS FOR DIFFERENT TYPES OF INGREDIENTS

STANDARD CUP	FINE POWDER (e.g. flour)	GRAIN (e.g. rice)	GRANULAR (e.g. sugar)	LIQUID SOLIDS (e.g. butter)	LIQUID (e.g. milk)
¾	105 g	113 g	143 g	150 g	180 ml
⅔	93 g	100 g	125 g	133 g	160 ml
½	70 g	75 g	95 g	100 g	120 ml
⅓	47 g	50 g	63 g	67 g	80 ml
¼	35 g	38 g	48 g	50 g	60 ml
⅛	18 g	19 g	24 g	25 g	30 ml

USEFUL EQUIVALENTS FOR LIQUID INGREDIENTS BY VOLUME

¼ tsp	=					1 ml
½ tsp	=					2 ml
1 tsp	=					5 ml
3 tsp	=	1 tbls	=	½ fl oz	=	15 ml
		2 tbls	=	⅛ cup	=	1 fl oz	=	30 ml
		4 tbls	=	¼ cup	=	2 fl oz	=	60 ml
		5⅓ tbls	=	⅓ cup	=	3 fl oz	=	80 ml
		8 tbls	=	½ cup	=	4 fl oz	=	120 ml
		10⅔ tbls	=	⅔ cup	=	5 fl oz	=	160 ml
		12 tbls	=	¾ cup	=	6 fl oz	=	180 ml
		16 tbls	=	1 cup	=	8 fl oz	=	240 ml
		1 pt	=	2 cups	=	16 fl oz	=	480 ml
		1 qt	=	4 cups	=	32 fl oz	=	960 ml
						33 fl oz	=	1000 ml = 1 L

USEFUL EQUIVALENTS FOR DRY INGREDIENTS BY WEIGHT
(To convert ounces to grams, multiply the number of ounces by 30.)

1 oz	=	$\frac{1}{16}$ lb	=	30 g
4 oz	=	¼ lb	=	120 g
8 oz	=	½ lb	=	240 g
12 oz	=	¾ lb	=	360 g
16 oz	=	1 lb	=	480 g

USEFUL EQUIVALENTS FOR COOKING/OVEN TEMPERATURES

	Fahrenheit	Celsius	Gas Mark
Freeze Water	32° F	0° C	
Room Temperature	68° F	20° C	
Boil Water	212° F	100° C	
Bake	325° F	160° C	3
	350° F	180° C	4
	375° F	190° C	5
	400° F	200° C	6
	425° F	220° C	7
	450° F	230° C	8
Broil			Grill

USEFUL EQUIVALENTS LENGTH
(To convert inches to centimeters, multiply the number of inches by 2.5.)

1 in	=			2.5 cm	
6 in	=	½ ft	=	15 cm	
12 in	=	1 ft	=	30 cm	
36 in	=	3 ft	= 1 yd	= 90 cm	
40 in	=			100 cm	= 1 m

THE GOOD HOUSEKEEPING
TRIPLE-TEST PROMISE

At *Good Housekeeping*, we want to make sure that every recipe we print works in any oven, with any brand of ingredient, no matter what. That's why, in our test kitchens at the **Good Housekeeping Research Institute**, we go all out: We test each recipe at least three times—and, often, several more times after that.

When a recipe is first developed, one member of our team prepares the dish, and we judge it on these criteria: It must be **delicious**, **family-friendly**, **healthy**, and **easy to make**.

1 The recipe is then tested several more times to fine-tune the flavor and ease of preparation, always by the same team member, using the same equipment.

2 Next, another team member follows the recipe as written, **varying the brands of ingredients** and **kinds of equipment**. Even the types of stoves we use are changed.

3 A third team member repeats the whole process **using yet another set of equipment** and **alternative ingredients**. By the time the recipes appear on these pages, they are guaranteed to work in any kitchen, including yours. **We promise**.